For Worship & Special Occasions

Group
Loveland, Colorado

Super Plays for Worship and Special Occasions
Copyright © 1994 Group Publishing, Inc.

Scriptures quoted from The Youth Bible, New Century Version, copyright © 1991 by Word Publishing, Dallas, Texas 75039. Used by permission.

Credits
Compiled by Mike Nappa
Edited by Mike Nappa and Paul Neale Lessard
Cover designed by Liz Howe
Cover illustrated by Greg Hargreaves
Interior designed by Joel Armstrong
Illustrations by Anita Dufalla
Special thanks to Chuck Bolte for his insightful evaluation of the plays in this book.

Library of Congress Cataloging-in-Publication Data
Super plays for worship and special occasions.
     p.   cm.
     Summary: A collection of twelve one-act plays on worship or special themes such as faith, the church, Easter, and new life in Christ.
     ISBN 1-55945-254-4
     1. Christian drama, American. 2. Young adult drama, American.
[1. Christian life--Drama. 2. Plays.] I. Group Publishing.
PS627.R4S83 1994
812'.04108382--dc20

                                                 94-27700
                                                   CIP
                                                      AC

10 9 8 7 6   03 02 01

Printed in the United States of America.

Visit our Web site: www.grouppublishing.com

Contents

INTRODUCTION
(Or How to Get a Standing Ovation Without Falling Flat on Your Face)

BY JULIANNE BRUCE

....

"In all the work you are doing, work the best you can. Work as if you were doing it for the Lord, not for people ... You are serving the Lord Christ" (COLOSSIANS 3:23-24).

Few mediums are as captivating as a well-performed play. The lights dim. A hush falls over the audience. Actors attempt to calm the butterflies in their stomachs. Almost without warning the curtain opens and characters come to life, presenting thoughts, ideas, and emotions through simple dialogue and a make-believe setting. Theater has enlightened and entertained audiences since the time of the ancient Greeks, when drama was the focus of religious ceremonies. In fact, theater was used exclusively by the church until the Middle Ages, when non-Christian drama came into its own. After its secularization, theater developed a bad reputation in some Christian circles, but today's churches are rediscovering drama as an effective means of communicating truth about God.

Christian theater provides a unique method for bringing a message to God's people. It allows members of a congregation to experience emotions and ideas from a safe distance, to face the challenges of life's problems and questions in a fictional setting. Then, based on that experience, they can draw new conclusions about their faith and the way they live the Christian life.

Christian theater also allows an opportunity for members of your youth group or adult congregation to join together in a creative, fun project. As they work to bring the performance to life, they'll learn about teamwork and commitment, and they'll experience the thrill of doing something significant for their church.

And you can make that happen.

No matter if your church is large or small, or rich or poor, you can use one of these *Super Plays for Worship and Special Occasions* to put on a great dramatic performance.

GETTING STARTED

The plays you are about to read are just that—plays. They're not long skits or short sketches that you can throw together at a moment's notice. Rather, they're full-fledged dramatic productions that will require planning, preparation, and rehearsals before you're ready for the performance. But don't let that scare you. The information in this chapter and the plays in this book are designed specifically for you. You'll find everything easy to use, practical to produce, and powerful in performance.

In addition, each play in this book is designed to be performed within a 20- to 30-minute time slot. That means you can use one of the plays from this book during a sermon time or as the focal point of another church-group meeting. Or you can prepare three of them for a night of one-act plays.

With *Super Plays for Worship and Special Occasions*, your church drama group doesn't need elaborate sets, Shakespearean actors, or Broadway glitz to put on a good show. You and your cast simply need a desire to present a message to God's people in a creative way and the commitment to make it happen.

Ready? Let's start planning!

PLANNING

Producing a church drama takes careful planning. Try following these three planning steps for your own production:

Step one: Selecting the play–Find a play in this book that suits the needs of your group. Look for a worship theme or special occasion that would be appropriate for production in your church. You'll also want to consider factors such as the number of characters needed, type of play, and complexity of set design.

Step two: The stage manager–Next, recruit an assistant—most often called the stage manager—who is second only to you, the director. This person needs to be organized, reliable, and resourceful because he or she will be responsible for getting props, helping with auditions, making copies, and anything else that may come up along the way. You might consider enlisting a responsible teenager from your youth group or another adult volunteer who has free time to commit to the production.

Step three: Creating the schedule–Once you've chosen your play and appointed a stage manager, you'll want to set a performance date. Find out who decides on themes or programs in your church—such as your senior pastor or church board. With that person or group, decide on the best time to put on the play, then write it into the official church-activities schedule. Be sure to allow yourself at least three to six months between the time you set the performance date and the actual performance.

Now you and your stage manager are ready to sit down and read through the chosen script. Read it several times so there's no doubt about what's involved in the play. Share thoughts and make notes about characters, props, themes—anything that comes to mind. Knowing the play well at this stage will save time in the long run.

Once you're both familiar with the play, it's time to create a schedule. Get a church calendar and work backwards from the day of the performance. You'll need to schedule every detail, making sure that auditions, set construction, and rehearsals don't interfere with other scheduled activities. Working through the sections in this chapter, you'll see what you need to include. When you've completed your schedule, submit it to anyone else who might need to schedule events so you'll avoid conflicts far in advance.

BLOCKING THE SCRIPT

Blocking is the plan for the movements your actors will make on stage, and it needs to be roughed out before the auditions. Stage directions (parenthetical remarks that explain how the writer envisioned the action or dialogue at that particular point) within the script do some blocking for you. Stage directions are excellent guidelines but rarely cover every move an actor will make. It's your job to decide how the rest of the action should be portrayed.

● **First, read through the script to get an idea of what you want your set to look like.** Then sketch it out on paper. It's easiest to draw the layout of the area where you are performing the play from an overhead perspective. Next, add the chairs, the doors, and so on to create a map of the set. You can use shapes such as squares or rectangles, with each one labeled as what it represents, to help you picture the stage area. For example, you might label triangles as "chair 1" and "chair 2," or you might label a rectangle as "bench."

● **Next, think through the basic blocking for your play.** Remember that every movement by your actors should have a purpose. It's distracting to have characters wander aimlessly but also boring for characters to remain motionless. The scene must be visually interesting. It's a delicate balance.

Consider what someone in the actor's position would normally do. Think about movements that would naturally correspond to what a character is saying. Ask yourself, "What does this line say that would cause Character X to move? In what way would he or she move?"

Write your blocking directions (in pencil) in your copy of the script. Once you see the movements done on stage you may change your mind, but at least you'll have a basic plan to go by.

● **Third, remember these general rules of thumb about blocking:** (1) don't do too much blocking or your actors will never remember it all, (2) an actor should never have his or her full back to the audience,

(3) don't form straight lines with your actors—break up the scene by staggering their positions, (4) don't let actors cross in front of each other, and (5) avoid having actors move while other actors are speaking.

AUDITIONS

For would-be actors *and* would-be directors, auditions are both an exhilarating and nerve-racking experience. In some churches every teenager in the youth group will be vying for the lead role. In other churches everyone will study their shoes while you ask for volunteers.

The key to holding successful auditions is to talk to people ahead of time. Go to Sunday school classes and youth meetings. Let people know what the play is about and what types of characters there are. Talk to parents. Put up posters and make announcements in the bulletins. Find out the main reasons people give for not trying out and advertise against them: "Bring a friend!" "No experience necessary!" Make phone calls to kids you think would do well and get them to audition. Don't take no for an answer. People will surprise themselves and you.

Many teenagers think they can't act or don't want to "look stupid." You'll have to convince them that theater is fun. The trick is to get them to the auditions. Once they've tried out for a part, they might just get hooked.

After you've set the audition date, you'll need to prepare several things. First, start praying about your choices. Ask God for guidance and wisdom to be able to make the best choices for the production.

Next, select materials for the auditions. Take the play you'll be performing and find short portions that allow for a wide range of emotions. The sections you choose should contain things such as a complete thought, a short conversation between two characters, or a paragraph from a monologue that expresses a concept. This will help your actors get a sense of what you want to see them do. Also include any blocking directions you've roughed out along with the scenes you choose.

Make certain that each character is in at least one of the scenes you choose so that you can audition people for any of the available roles. Once you've made your choices, photocopy those sections for as many characters as appear in that portion. The prospective actors will use those to read from during auditions. Also make copies for the stage manager and for yourself so that you won't have to fumble with a full script during the audition.

If you have more than 20 people auditioning, it might be best to have two audition times. If it's a group of 10 or fewer, have them meet at an assigned place and time. While there is no need to give out scripts before the audition date, you can give people the chance to read over the photocopied portions before they begin the audition.

When people show up for the auditions, have them fill out sheets that give their vital information. You can use the "Audition Information Sheet" on page 16 or make one of your own.

If you create your own audition information sheets, they should include name, address, phone number, grade, previous experience, and, most importantly, times they're available to rehearse. Across the bottom of the page make a simple, seven-day calendar on which the kids can indicate times that they are available. Also include an area where they can write one-time conflicts such as dental appointments, sports camps, or family vacations. Ask for these sheets at the beginning of the audition, then you can write your comments on the back. This way the information won't get separated.

When the auditions begin, have several different people read for any parts they might be right for. It's fine to try different combinations of actors but don't make anyone wait around unless you know you'll want to use them again. If you think you might want someone to read again later, tell them why you're having them wait. Otherwise, try to get the entire audition over for each person as soon as possible.

To audition someone, first introduce yourself and your stage manager. Then explain the play in a couple of sentences. Tell them who the characters are and how they relate to the action. Don't be afraid to tell them just what you want to accomplish with the scenes. Have each person read at least two scenes so you can get an idea of his or her skills. Don't be afraid to have actors read several scenes if you need to. Sometimes people need the chance to get past their nervousness.

As people read for different parts, use the back of their "Audition Information Sheets" to take notes. Write down the outstanding characteristics of each person auditioning, such as "long red hair" or "very tall." This will help you to remember unfamiliar people.

Also write down outstanding features of each person's acting ability, as well as your observations. No one will see these, so you should be frank. Indicate things such as "good projection," "follows direction well," "presents herself in a believable way," "slow reader but might improve with practice," "no emotion," and so on.

Jot down whatever will help you remember that person and his or her abilities. Keep in mind that some people improve with practice. Look for potential. Then list any roles they might be appropriate for. Your stage manager should do the same so you can compare notes at the end of the process.

At the end of the audition tell everyone when you'll make your decisions and where you'll post the cast list (a list that tells who you've chosen for each role).

Next, meet with your stage manager and select the people you'd

like to play the roles in the production. If possible, select understudies for each role as well. Then you'll have backups in case of sickness, injury, or someone dropping out.

Decide on the role assignments as soon as possible after the auditions. That way you'll remember the details of each actor, and kids don't have to wait too long to find out whether they made the play or not. Generally it's best to make your decisions within two or three days of the auditions.

Remember to be especially careful about checking availability when making your casting decisions. Coordinating schedules is tricky, so don't schedule people who can't meet at the same time. You'll end up losing. Be ready to sacrifice a good combination for one that will be practical. Also, encourage those who might not ordinarily feel comfortable in the spotlight by giving them minor roles when available.

When you're ready, type out your cast list. Include on it a schedule of the rehearsal dates and an encouraging note at the bottom thanking everyone who participated in the auditions. Post it in a prominent place in the church so that everyone involved can find it easily.

After the cast list goes up, call those who didn't get a role to see if they would still like to be involved. There's always need for extra help. Be sure to give them titles and make them a part of the production so they don't feel as if they got stuck doing something no one else wanted to do. For example, you may select a prop coordinator, sound technician, stage hand, and so on.

SETS, PROPS, COSTUMES, AND MAKEUP

Now that you have selected your cast and crew, it's time to determine what you'll do for sets, props, and costumes.

Glance over the script to see what materials it calls for, then make a list of everything you'll need for the performance. Next, with your stage manager, check your church's resources to see what's available to you.

Check your church's resource or crafts room, members of the congregation, at thrift stores and flea markets, or friends and family to find the needed materials for your sets, props, and costumes. Take care not to borrow anything that's irreplaceable and make sure to return everything immediately after the show—in its original condition.

On rare occasions when a particular item isn't available, you'll want to explore items you can substitute. For example, if a script calls for tricycles but none are available, you might substitute wagons, skateboards, or bicycles instead.

• **Sets—**The plays in this book call for relatively simple sets, but if you have a large budget or willing and capable people who can build elaborate sets, feel free to use them. Visit your local library to find resources on how to build flats (the large backdrops in plays) and other necessary equipment. However, keep in mind that sets can take weeks to build and are difficult to move. Make sure that the elaborate set is worth the cost in time, space, and effort before proceeding.

If your church can't afford even the minimal set requested in your chosen play, consider using a modern theater convention—the bare stage. Exact representations aren't necessary. Theater is based on suspension of disbelief. The audience knows they are in the sanctuary or gymnasium, and not even an elaborate set can change that. If you give them just a few hints about the location, most people are willing to pretend they are somewhere else. A backdrop is rarely even necessary. A table with two chairs and a napkin holder can suggest a kitchen. Unless the script calls for an actor to put something in an oven, it's not necessary to have one. Even then, the actor can pantomime the activity or go offstage to do it. Audience members will fill in the details with their imaginations.

● **Props**–Simplicity is also a good rule for props. Numerous props equal numerous problems. Don't overwhelm your actors or your acting space. Everything onstage should have a purpose. If the script doesn't call for an actor to make a pot of coffee, he or she probably doesn't need to.

Since many people will be using the props, it's best if you or your stage manager takes charge of gathering the props and checking them out during rehearsals. Make a list of the props and keep everything in one place between rehearsals.

● **Costumes**–Full costumes can add to a performance but aren't absolutely necessary, either. Suggestions work well here, too. For example, an elderly character can wear an old-style hat and a loose jacket that allows him or her to hunch over and carry a cane. Gray hair and wrinkles aren't necessary.

Also, your actors needn't look glamorous unless a glamorous character appears in the script. These are characters, so have some fun with them. An actor playing a child can look silly with mismatched patterns as though he dressed himself. An actress playing a stereotypical '60s era housewife can wear her hair in pink rollers with a hideous scarf tied over them.

To save time, have your actors be responsible for finding their own costumes. Let them know at the first rehearsal what you want them to wear and have them start gathering the clothes right away. They'll be better at finding their own sizes and will know more places to look. Once costumes are ready, keep them together in the place where you store your props.

● **Makeup**–Since stark white light tends to wash out people's color, using makeup can help define your actors' faces, especially in a large church. If someone in the church is able to do stage makeup, it'll add a nice touch to the performance. But remember, makeup is best used to enhance the actors' faces a bit, not change their appearance completely.

Have females simply apply their eye makeup, blush, and lipstick somewhat heavier than usual—about twice as much. If they're willing, have males use a bit of blush, some mascara, and a light-colored lipstick. (Ask the girls to help them apply it, if it's appropriate.) Be sure to plan one or two full-makeup rehearsals so you can check that the makeup looks appropriate on stage.

LIGHT AND SOUND

● **Light-**All you *really* need in the way of lighting is the ability to turn off the house lights (the lights above the audience) and leave the stage area lit. This type of lighting will direct the audience's attention to the right area. If you have a "follow-spot" (a large spot light that shines a circle of colored light), you can use it together with normal church lighting to highlight one actor during a speech, or you can use it as the sole source of light.

If your church's lighting capabilities are greater, see what you can accomplish with light and sound. If your church has an elaborate setup, find out who's in charge and talk with that person. He or she can guide you through the ins and outs of what your system can do. See if you can change lighting colors and intensities or have the ability to make lights fade up and down on cue. You can use those techniques to add emphasis or changes in mood during the performance.

● **Sound-**Microphones help your actors to project their voices in a clear, loud way. Even if you place microphones on the stage in front of the acting space, they are usually a minimal distraction. Recruit a stage hand to operate the sound-control board. Have this person be in charge of setting up and tearing down the sound equipment and adjusting the volume levels during the performance.

REHEARSALS

Plan to start rehearsals soon after auditions but give your actors enough time to work out their schedules.

The amount of rehearsals needed will vary with the play, the skills of the actors, and the level of performance you are looking for. Generally, one or two rehearsals a week for two months should give you sufficient time to prepare for the production. During the last week before the performance, however, you'll want to schedule at least three rehearsals. Make sure one is a technical rehearsal (a rehearsal where the actors work with technicians in charge of lights, sound, and any other technical aspects of the play) and one is a dress rehearsal (a rehearsal with everything, as if it were the actual performance).

Don't plan more than two or three hours for any one rehearsal and be aware that your actors may have schoolwork or other commitments in addition to the play. Usually weekend afternoons work best for rehearsals, but check with your cast and crew to determine the times that work best for your group.

Remind your cast and crew that as you get closer to the performance date, you may need to schedule more rehearsal time. It'll simply depend on their progress and commitment.

Before the first rehearsal, give your actors their scripts. Tell them to read through the play several times to become familiar with it.

• **The First Rehearsal–**At the first rehearsal, ask your cast members what they want to accomplish with this play. As a group, have them set a goal so that you're all working toward the same objective. For example, a goal might be "To challenge people to live out their Christian faith every day" or "To give people a new appreciation for the new life that Jesus gives."

You'll also want to do a read-through of the play. Have actors stand on the stage and read their parts until they've gone through the whole script. Allow them to move wherever feels natural for them. Keep an eye out for any good, new blocking ideas the actors come up with and jot them down.

After the read-through, have the cast explore the roles they're playing. Tell actors to suggest characteristics of the people they're portraying. For example, an actor might say, "I picture this character as the type of person who likes danger. She probably rides a motorcycle and loves the fast rides at amusement parks." Or a cast member might say, "My character is a clerk at the fast-food restaurant. He clenches his fists a lot because he's got a lot of anger about how he's treated at work. That's why he's so mean to others." This will help the cast make connections with their characters and will give the performance depth.

Encourage your actors to start memorizing early. Give them an absolute deadline—no exceptions. There's nothing worse than having actors stare blankly at one another during the performance, while your audience checks their watches wondering if they'll get home in time for a rerun on television. You'll probably have to call your actors and remind them a couple of times before the deadline, just to be sure.

Close the first rehearsal with a group prayer. Encourage your cast to pray for you, for themselves, and for the audience during the coming weeks. Prayer will guide your production and bond your group. Prayer also creates unity among your production team.

• **The Second Rehearsal–**During the second rehearsal, give your actors the blocking. Go through the play line by line and tell your actors where they should move and why. Have cast members write all of the blocking in their scripts (in pencil) so they are aware of where other actors are going to be. Then have them do a read-through of the script with the blocking. Don't be picky at this point. Just allow them to get a general feel for it.

Again remind actors about your deadline for memorizing lines and check on cast members' progress. Close your second rehearsal with prayer, asking God for help to complete the task set before you.

• **The Third Rehearsal–**During the third rehearsal, run through the play with the blocking to see how it flows. Take opportunities to make changes or suggestions at this point. Encourage actors to begin working without their scripts.

The purpose of this rehearsal is to start making the play seem like a play. Characters will begin to develop as you work through the scenes, and the cast will start to feel as though they are really working on a project.

Rerun scenes or the entire play as often as time allows. Be sure to close with group prayer.

● **Subsequent Rehearsals–**During subsequent rehearsals, take one section of the play at a time to work on. Go through line by line, stopping actors as often as necessary to guide them in the right tone of voice or movement. Don't push them, though. They're trying. If an actor seems frustrated, go on. Make yourself a note to work on that portion later. Some parts will go more smoothly than others. Rerun the parts that need work as often as necessary.

Get your actors "off book" (not using the script) as soon as possible. Have your stage manager be the prompter—the person who tells the actors the lines if they forget them. If someone does forget, tell him or her to say "line" as a signal for the stage manager to read the line. Then continue the scene. Getting actors "off book" quickly will help memorization, and the cast will have an easier time acting without trying to hold on to the scripts.

Encourage your actors to be "bigger than life" in their portrayals. This does not mean melodramatic, but the emotions must carry. Push the actors until they almost feel silly. You'll hear complaints, but it's at that point when they're just beginning to emote enough. This is especially true with emotions like anger and joy. A play has emotional levels that rise and fall. Each time there is a change, it needs to be apparent to the audience, or the performance will seem flat.

Help your actors work on their projection, too. If you don't have microphones, make sure the people in the back of the church can still hear. During rehearsals sit in various locations around the sanctuary (or where the audience will be) to see if the audience will be able to hear your actors well. Projection does not mean screaming; it means pushing the words and emotions out toward the audience in a clear, sustained, and forceful way. If your actors are having problems, contact the choir director for tips. Singers must project, and the director can explain to your cast how to accomplish this.

As soon as the majority of the play seems to be going well, start running it through in its entirety. Once you get a rhythm going in a rehearsal, allow the actors to go on without interruption. Things will start to flow. Take notes to give the cast after the run-through. Then they can run it again, following your suggestions. Start to give them as much rein as possible as soon as you can.

Don't forget to cheer your cast as well as give suggestions for how they can improve. Praise will get you better results than harsh criticism. If your actors start to feel self-conscious or bad about their acting, they'll only get worse. Keep your suggestions pleasant, not cruel.

● **The Technical Rehearsal–**If you're going to have people run lights and/or sound, schedule time for them to practice their parts of the show before the technical rehearsal. Then, the week before the performance, run a technical rehearsal where the technical crew and the actors work together to eliminate any last minute bugs, such as low microphone levels, glaring lights, and so on.

Warn actors that this technical rehearsal might be difficult. It can be hard to get lights set and sound levels right on the first try. Make sure your technical crew has scripts with their cues marked. Have the actors run through the parts where the technical crew has something to do. Do each light or sound change several times until the technical people have a feel for it—even if it's just turning the main lights off and on. It'll make a big difference at performance time.

● **The Dress Rehearsal–**This is it. The last chance to get it right. No stopping; no starting over. This rehearsal is usually scheduled the day before the performance, though if you have time you can schedule several dress rehearsals before the performance date. Run through the play no matter what the mistakes. It should be just like a real performance. Make notes only on major problems. Give last-minute suggestions at the end of the performance. And remember, there's a tradition in the theater that a bad dress rehearsal means a great performance.

PROGRAMS

Two weeks before the performance, make up programs. Put the title of the play and an interesting design or picture on the front. Use the people in the church office as a resource for this kind of project.

The program has a twofold purpose. First, it lets the audience know what to expect, so include dates and times your production will start, a sequence of scenes (if applicable), and a brief summary of what the play will be about. Second, it provides a way to recognize the people who helped with the production. Find a place in the program to appreciate everyone—even if each person helped out only in minor ways. Nobody wants to be ignored after he or she has given time and effort to a project.

THE PERFORMANCE

On the day of the performance, have the cast and crew arrive two hours before the show starts. That'll give them time to change clothes, set up, and make any last-minute preparations. Be sure cast and crew members know where they should be before going on stage and when they should be ready. Just before the performance starts, pray together one last time.

This will put the performance in the right perspective, and it will help to calm and focus everyone.

Be sure to have some sort of ending or curtain call planned for the play. The actors should freeze after the last line while the stage lights are brought down (turned off). If a pastor wants to end the play and continue the service with a short message, bring the stage lights down and have the actors file off stage while the pastor begins the next portion of the service. If a curtain call is appropriate, bring the lights back up and have the cast move into a line at the front of the stage area. They should take a bow simultaneously, then file offstage.

After the show, plan some kind of celebration for your cast and crew as a way to say thanks for a job well done. You might host a pizza party, go to a late movie, or simply go to a cast member's house for snacks.

Now you're ready. Break a leg!

Audition Information Sheet

Name _____

Address _____

Phone Number _____ Grade in School _____

Previous Dramatic Experience _____

_____

_____

_____

_____

_____

Times you're available to rehearse
(write times on the appropriate days below):

Sunday _____

_____

Monday _____

_____

Tuesday _____

_____

Wednesday _____

_____

Thursday _____

_____

Friday _____

_____

Saturday _____

_____

One-time conflicts you know of that might affect your rehearsal or performance schedule (such as a dental appointments, sports camp, or family vacations):

Date_____ Conflict _____

Date_____ Conflict _____

Date_____ Conflict _____

THE CONVERSION OF A PREACHER MAN

BY JODY WAKEFIELD BROLSMA

....
" 'Be careful! When you do good things, don't do them in front
of people to be seen by them. If you do that, you will have no
reward from your Father in heaven' "
(MATTHEW 6:1).

THEME

Faith for every day.

SUMMARY

A visit from a heavenly messenger changes Trev's idea of sharing one's faith.

CHARACTERS

Trev Rogers–He's a young math teacher with a Barney Fife-ish attitude about his Christianity.

Pastor–This person needs a good preaching voice.

Lynette–A history teacher.

Paul–An English teacher.

Angela–A young Spanish teacher.

Dan–The school janitor, he is a little older, gruff, and grumpy.

Messenger–A female, similar in build and age to Angela, she is aggressive, with a sense of humor. (This part could be played by the same person who is Angela.)

Teachers–Two to four anonymous teachers act as background extras in the teachers lounge.

SETTING

Most of the action takes place in the teachers lounge at school, where there are tables, chairs, posters, a coffee pot, plastic cups, and stacks of papers. Trev's room need only consist of a bed (or something similar) and a night stand with an alarm clock on it. His bedroom can be set to the far side of stage left.

PROPS

A Bible, Christian tracts (from a distance, any brochure will do), book bags or briefcases, books, a radio with headphones, a white baseball cap with a large cross drawn or pinned to the front, a tie, a broom, garbage cans with plastic liners, and taped organ music. You'll also need appropriate stage lights and sound.

THE SCRIPT
"The Conversion of a Preacher Man"

(Stage is dark except for spotlight on Trev, who is sitting in a chair in the teachers lounge area and holding his Bible. He's dressed for work in a shirt

and tie; looking up, as if listening to someone. From offstage, Pastor's voice begins.)

Pastor: And that's why Jesus says, "You are the light of the world." We need to shine out God's light in everything we do, in everything we say, in everything we are, each and every day. Jesus didn't say, "You are the light of the world...sometimes" or "You are the light of the world when you feel like it." He said, "You are the light of the world." Period. *(Pauses.)* As we close with the final verse of "O the Deep, Deep Love of Jesus," ask yourself, "Am I shining out God's light in everything I do?" "Am I being a light to MY world?"

(Organ music plays softly.)

Trev: *(Prays looking up, as if talking to God.)* Dear God, help me to be a light to the people in my world...even though I'm not sure how. I mean, God, I'm not exactly "light" material. You see me mess up all the time. *(Smiles.)* But you still love me. I guess that's what I want people to know—that you love them no matter what. But as far as this "being-a-light" thing...I'm not sure how. I try to show people that I'm a Christian, but...

(Lights go up and teachers rush into lounge, laughing, talking, and joking around. Some are grabbing papers and rushing out; others are sitting down with cups of coffee. A bell rings and the lounge clears except for Trev, Lynette, Paul, and a few other teachers, who are grading papers, reading, or chatting quietly. Trev greets a few teachers, then bumps into Lynette.)

Trev: Lynette, I heard that your guest speaker last Friday was great! Kids came into class raving about Mrs. Merriam's Civil War general.

Lynette: He was great all right, until he told the class that soldiers in the Civil War dropped out of school to join the Army. I had three seniors get up to go enlist!

Trev: *(Laughing)* Seniors will do anything to get out of school! Hey, how was your weekend? I heard that your parents were going to be in town.

Lynette: Yeah, it was good to see them again. I really miss them, and it's so expensive to fly out there. Sometimes I wish that Tyler and Katie could see more of their grandparents, but it's just been hard lately.

Trev: Yeah, I know how that can be. I really miss my parents, too. *(Reaches for a baseball cap, which he keeps in his back pocket or tucked into his waistband.)* What with them being born-again-Christian missionaries in Africa spreading the good news about Jesus to all the primitive tribes there, starting new churches, translating the Bible into native languages, and leading four Bible studies, they don't get home much. I just remember to "kneel in my prayer-closet and lift up their souls to God" for a few hours each night. That makes them seem closer.

Lynette: *(Rolls eyes and gets up.)* That's a...uh...great idea, Trev. I'll remember it. I need to make a phone call. *(Exits quickly.)*

(Trev takes off cap and goes to the coffee pot for a refill. Paul is leaning against the wall reading a book.)

Trev: Hi, Paul. How's it going?

Paul: *(Looks up from book.)* Good, as far as Mondays go.

Trev: Some good reading there?

Paul: Yeah, it's Matthew Crider's newest book. I've been trying to finish it for weeks, but it's tough to find the time. You should read it, it's incredible.

Trev: I'd love to, but *(putting cap back on)* I spend most of my reading time digging into God's Word. My day just isn't complete unless I've drunk the sweet milk of Scripture for a few hours. But for lighter reading, I've found that these "Tracts of Truth" are excellent, too. *(Pulls out tracts.)* Why don't you take one and let me know what you think.

Paul: *(Moving to a chair, focusing on the book)* I'm pretty busy with this book. But thanks anyway. *(Turns attention to book.)*

Trev: OK, well, praise the Lord!

(Trev removes his cap and takes his coffee to the table, where he sits down to grade some papers. After a few seconds, Angela enters with a book.)

Angela: Hi, Trev.

Trev: Oh hi, Angela. How's life in freshman Spanish?

Angela: Bueno, bueno! Today's extra credit day, so the kids are bringing in Mexican food. I'm stuffed! I think next year I'll have them write stories in Spanish—it'd be less fattening!

(Both laugh.)

Angela: Hey, speaking of food, we missed you at the faculty dessert last week. Where were you?

(Other teachers in room groan.)

Trev: *(Puts on cap.)* Oh, I was strengthening my spirit at the 10th Annual Born-Again-Christian Revival and Renewal Meeting. Didn't you get a flier? I put them in everyone's box last Monday.

Angela: Uh…no…I guess not.

Trev: Well, that's OK, because I go to three "Diggin'-Deep-in-the-Word" Bible studies each week. You can come to one of those instead. We're studying spiritual gifts in one, the fruit of the Spirit in another, and the book of Hebrews in the third. Sounds fascinating, right?

Angela: I-I'm not sure.

Trev: If you don't have a Bible, I can loan you one. I've got three of each version.

Angela: It's not that. It's just that I'm really busy at home these days. Things have been tight, so I'm doing some bookkeeping for my brother's company in the evenings. I miss the time with my kids, but it's helping make ends meet. So Bible study is pretty much out.

Trev: I see. *(Starts to remove hat, changes mind.)* How about reading one of these "Tracts of Truth" instead? They're really short—it'll hardly take any time at all! Here's one I think you'll really enjoy.

Angela: Well, OK. I can't promise you that I'll have the time to read it or anything. But, thanks just the same.

Trev: No problem. And remember, praise the Lord!

(Everyone freezes in the teachers lounge. Lights fade on lounge, then go up on Trev's bedroom. Trev enters, sets down briefcase, and throws cap on the bed. He takes off his shirt and tie, revealing a white T-shirt underneath. He sits on the bed and takes off his shoes, then puts on a baggy pajama shirt over his T-shirt.)

Trev: What a day! Christianity is tiring, God! There are so many people who need you. I mean, like Angela. She's alone in the city, raising two kids on her own, struggling financially, and just seems so lonely. If only I could show her that knowing you helps fill in all those gaps, that walking with you makes life...different. I try, Lord, honestly, but for some reason, nobody ever wants to listen. Maybe if I practice...(*Picks up cap, tucks it in his waistband, and stands in front of imaginary mirror. Practices putting it on, as if in a quick-draw shootout. Talks confidently to mirror.*) Hi, I'm a born-again-know-where-I've-been-now-headed-to-Heaven Christian. (*"Draws" his cap again.*) Do you know Jesus? He knows you! (*Draws his cap once more.*) I want you to know I've spent hours kneeling in my prayer-closet lifting up your very soul to God. (*Leaves the cap on; quick-draws a tract.*) May I share about God with you? Praise the Lord! (*Takes off cap and tosses it on the bed.*) Aw, I don't know. Something's just not right. How can I make people see you, God?

(Discouraged, Trev crawls into bed. Lights dim. After a few seconds, the Messenger enters. She's wearing a white mask that covers her eyes and nose, baggy white sweats, a white baseball cap, and high-top sneakers. She wears a whistle around her neck, which she blows loudly. Trev jumps.)

Trev: Wha...

Messenger: Trev Rogers, right?

Trev: Yeah, but, who're...what're you...how'd...what's going on?

Messenger: Take it easy, Trev. You and I just need to have a little chat. Your Father asked me to come down and help you out. Explain a few new ground rules, go over...

Trev: (*Interrupting*) Dad? How do you know my dad? Did he give you a key to get in here? Help me with what? Who are you?

Messenger: Of course I know your dad! A wonderful man, but not the topic of our little tête-à-tête. I'm referring to your FATHER (*pointing upward*), you know, your HEAVENLY Father.

Trev: You mean...(*Looks up, then looks at Messenger.*)

Messenger: (*Nodding*) The one and only!

Trev: Then that would make you a—that means you're an...

Messenger: Yep. And a very busy one, so let's get down to business.

Trev: But wait, shouldn't you have wings or something? And what about your halo?

Messenger: The wing thing was scratched years ago. They kept getting tangled up in telephone lines. Same with the halos. (*Pointing to baseball cap*) These are much more comfy—wash and wear—a life saver in case of a bad-hair day... (*Looking up suddenly*) Oh, sorry, back to business.

Trev: Just a minute. (*Reaches for his cap, which is laying on the floor.*)

Messenger: (*Grabs it before he can.*) Uh, uh, uh. (*Shaking head*) That's just what I'm here to talk about.

Trev: But I'm trying! I'll get faster, I promise. I've always been slower than everyone else. Even back in third grade in Mrs. Reinebach's class, when everyone else was learning their multiplication tables, I was still...

Messenger: Brushing up on your subtraction. Yes, I know. But that's not what I'm here about. (*Holding up cap*) Trev, this isn't what shows people that you're a child of God. (*Picking up tracts from night stand*) Neither do these! And especially not your long-winded speeches about what an amazing Christian you are.

Trev: But I'm supposed to be a light, shining out God's love.

Messenger: Yes, but you're not supposed to BLIND people!

Trev: So what am I supposed to do?

Messenger: Well, first of all, get rid of these things. (*Tosses cap and tracts offstage.*) Whew, I feel worlds better already, don't you?

Trev: (*Looking longingly offstage*) Well, actually...

Messenger: Now stand up straight.

(*Trev stands at attention.*)

Messenger: Look me in the eyes. Do you feel like a child of God?

Trev: (*Relaxes, looking down*) In my pajamas?

Messenger: In your pajamas, in a clown suit, in a dress... who cares?

Trev: Well, I'd feel pretty ridiculous in a dress...

Messenger: Trev! Listen to me! Your faith lives in here (*touching Trev's chest*), not out here (*picking up the tie from where Trev dropped it*).

Trev: (*Discouraged*) Aw, I knew I'd get it all wrong. I'm a flop at being a Christian. Why can't I be like those guys at church who always have it together? They're never late for service; they teach Sunday school, lead Bible studies, support missionaries, and tell all their co-workers about Christ...

Messenger: And that's why two of those guys are next on my list for a visit this evening. They've got their own problems, too.

Trev: (*Mouth drops.*) No!

Messenger: Yes! Now would you listen up? Time's a-wastin', and I have an idea that those two visits are going to be even tougher. (*Under her breath*) What a night!

Trev: You've got to be kidding! If THOSE guys have problems, I'm really messed up.

Messenger: (*Sighing*) Trev, Trev, Trev. We're going to try something different. (*Turns him toward bed.*) Crawl back into bed and go to sleep.

Trev: (*Getting under covers*) I'm such an awful Christian that you're giving up on me?

Messenger: No, you're not an awful Christian. You love God and really want others to know him, too. Your heart is perfect! So, that's what I'm going to leave you with tomorrow. No tracts, no Bible, no long speeches, no missionary letters. Just your heart.

Trev: (*Yawns.*) Just...my heart?

Messenger: (*Chuckling to herself as Trev falls asleep*) The cold-turkey method. It's a toughie, but it works every time. Poor guy won't know what hit him in the morning. (*Checking watch*) And now for the real challenge—two ultra-super Christians with faith as thin as a choir robe. (*Looking to heaven*) You love giving me these, don't you? (*Walking offstage*) Yeah, yeah, I know.

(*Stage lights dim for a few seconds, then brighten. Trev's alarm goes off—an egg timer will work for a sound effect. Trev turns the alarm off, sits up, yawns, and stretches.*)

Trev: What a night! I had the weirdest dream—an angel in a sweat suit came and told me I had to teach multiplication to some people at church. (*Confused look*) Or something like that. Oh well. Better get ready for work. (*Reaches for cap on night stand but can't find it.*) Where in the world...(*Looks around room.*) Hmmm, maybe I put it with my tracts. (*Opens night stand drawer, but it's empty. Begins searching frantically.*) They're gone! Someone stole all of my tracts! (*Stops and thinks.*) But then they'd read them and might become Christians, which would actually be a good thing. (*Frantic again*) But what am I supposed to do? My missionary letters were with them, too, so I can't even show those off. Wait! Where's my Bible? You're kidding! Someone stole my Bible? What kind of a person would steal a Bible? I mean, really! You just can't trust...(*Stops. Sits on bed.*) The angel. I remember the angel. In my dream, the angel took all my...Then that means that my dream...wasn't a dream.

(*Lights go out on Trev's room. Lights go up on teachers lounge. A few teachers are bustling around, getting papers, grabbing a quick cup of coffee to take to class, or stapling papers together. Paul enters, sits down, and begins grading a stack of papers. The bell rings, and all but a few teachers clear out. Lynette enters carrying a radio with headphones.*)

Lynette: Assigned too much homework, I see.

Paul: (*Shaking head*) I remember when I thought being a teacher would be easy—no homework. These English essays take forever to grade!

Lynette: Why the rush to get them graded? This is your break period.

Paul: I'm going to my little brother's bachelor party tonight. I'd hate to be grading an English essay when they bring out Lola, the Belly-Dancing Legend.

Lynette: Stop! I don't want to hear any more about what goes on at a bachelor party! My husband had one, and it's probably better that I remain in the dark.

Paul: (*Laughing*) OK. Anyway, tonight's out, and tomorrow I'm sure I'll have a headache the size of Mount Rushmore from all the...

(*Trev enters, looking a little out of it. Paul stops talking and goes back to his papers. Lynette starts to put her headphones on but stops when she notices how odd Trev looks.*)

Lynette: Trev? Are you OK?

Trev: Yeah. (*Reaches for his back pocket but then remembers. Smiles nervously.*) Fine.

Lynette: You look...different. I mean, it's a good kind of different but definitely...different. Did you get a haircut or something?

Trev: No, it's just that...well, it must be that I was up all night praising the L...(*Trev is overcome by a coughing fit, cutting off his sentence. When he recovers, he continues.*) As I was saying, I was up all night...(*short cough*) pr-practicing my tuba. (*Intended to say "praising the Lord" but the words came out wrong. With a quizzical look, he mouths "practicing my tuba" to the audience.*)

Lynette: (*Slowly*) Practicing your...tuba? Why? I mean, I didn't even know you played the tuba?

Trev: Um, well, it's something I've just recently—really recently—taken up.

Lynette: Great, well maybe if you keep practicing hard you'll be able to play something at the faculty Christmas party.

Paul: Christmas party? Trev, I don't think you've been to a faculty Christmas party in three years.

Trev: Yeah (*thinking aloud*), not since I became a born-again-know-where-I've-been...(*coughing fit again*) Whew! Excuse me. I meant to say, not since I became a Chri..(*short cough*) Chr-chrysanthemum. (*Meant to say Christian, realizes what he said and tries to recover.*) Uh...freak! A chrysanthemum freak! (*Beginning to sweat a bit*) I spend all of my time cultivating my garden and growing...chrysanthemums.

(*Paul and Lynette look at each other oddly.*)

Paul: I'd think you could take a night off to go to a party.

Lynette: You could even bring some of your flowers for decoration.

Trev: Sure. I...uh...guess I'd never thought of that. (*Changing the topic*) Say, has anyone seen Angela today? I gave her a tr...I gave her something to read, and I wanted to talk to her about it.

Paul: You haven't heard?

Trev: Heard what?

Lynette: She transferred to North Central High. I guess it's closer to her house and her kids' school.

Paul: She'd been wanting to transfer for a while, but there wasn't an opening for a Spanish teacher. George Beardsley said that North Central called yesterday and asked for her after their Spanish teacher quit. It's kind of a tough area. She's got her work cut out for her.

Trev: (*In his most holy-sounding voice*) Well, then, I'd better kneel in my closet and pr-…(*short cough*) pr-prune for her. (*Covering his mistake*) Uh…I mean…prune my chrysanthemums. (*Pauses.*) So I can take her some flowers. To encourage her.

Lynette: Trev, that's so thoughtful. I know that would mean a lot to Angela. She'll need all the encouragement she can get.

Paul: (*Standing up*) Look, you two, you're not helping me get this work done. I'll be in the library. (*Starts to leave, then turns around.*) And, Trev, good luck on the tuba practice. (*Exits.*)

Lynette: Well, if you don't mind, I'm going to relax with Bach for the remainder of this all-too-short break. (*Puts on headphones and relaxes in a chair or on the couch.*)

Trev: (*To himself*) Great. I've succeeded in making a complete idiot of myself. Plus I'm expected to bring chrysanthemums to every occasion and play "Frosty the Snowman" on the tuba. (*Pauses.*) But, it was kind of nice to have people talk to me…almost as if they liked me.

(*Dan enters and changes the liners in the trash cans, then sweeps the floor.*)

Dan: How's the preacher man today?

Trev: (*Wryly*) Not preaching today, I'm afraid.

Dan: (*Sarcastically*) Well, praise the Lord.

Trev: (*Smiling*) Great to have you back, Dan. I missed your words of encouragement last week.

Dan: Humph!

Trev: So how was the vacation?

Dan: (*Doesn't look up.*) Dandy.

Trev: What'd you see? Where'd you go?

Dan: Went to Florida. Saw my folks.

Trev: Sounds…great. (*Starts to say something but decides against it. Opens briefcase and gets out a stack of papers. There should be a few seconds of silence.*)

Dan: (*Still sweeping*) My dad…died.

(*Trev reaches for his hat, out of habit, but stops and runs his fingers through his hair. Pauses.*)

Trev: (*Slowly*) I'm sorry. You must feel…sad.

Dan: He was a good man. (*Looks up from sweeping.*) A real good man. Gonna miss him.

Trev: (*Softly*) I know.

Dan: *(Takes a deep breath.)* Well, looks like I'm done in here. Gotta stopped-up toilet in the boys locker room. Someone tried to flush a freshman. *(Starts to leave.)*

Trev: Dan?

(Dan stops, turns around. Trev looks toward heaven, then at Dan.)

Trev: I'll be . . . I'll be praying for you.

Dan: *(Pauses, then nods.)* Sure. *(Exits.)*

(Lights go out except for a spotlight on Angela, now dressed in the Messenger's outfit.)

Angela: *(Speaking to God)* Yeah, you're right. He's gonna be OK. Just got caught up a bit much in the Christian-cliché thing. *(Takes off mask.)* Now for this North Central High assignment; we need to talk! There's this guy—yes, I know you know him—and he's got this problem . . .

(Walks offstage talking. Lights go out.)

THE END

THE HEART OF THE RACE

BY JULIANNE BRUCE

"We have around us many people whose lives tell us what faith means. So let us run the race that is before us and never give up. We should remove from our lives anything that would get in the way and the sin that so easily holds us back" **(HEBREWS 12:1).**

THEME
The Church.

SUMMARY
This allegory humorously depicts the people of a church as members of a tricycle-racing team who have trouble agreeing on the best way to get started.

CHARACTERS
The Reverend Coach–He is a man of faith who tries to lead by example. He doesn't want to tell all the answers but would rather lead the other racers to greater understanding.

Kristin–She is anxious to get started racing and feels that her teammates' ideas could be handled just as easily while they are in motion. She believes the tricycles will keep them going and doesn't think racers should worry about the particulars until problems come up.

Marcus–He loves the look of his tricycle far more than actually being in the race. He wants to stay with it and care for it. He's not very interested in moving because he's afraid it might mess up the looks of the tricycle.

Kyrie–Kyrie is new to tricycles and tricycle racing. She isn't even sure how to begin riding. She looks for direction from the others and tries to imitate them in order to understand how it's done.

Tyler–He is embarrassed by his tricycle. He tries to hide the trike and doesn't want to talk about it openly, except to wonder if a tricycle is really for him. He ignores the problems with his tricycle because he doesn't want to admit to having it.

Kent–He's been a racer for a long time and thinks he's got all the answers. He'd rather sit back and talk about his vast knowledge than race.

Narrator–This person opens and closes the play.

SETTING
The play is set in the locker room of a racing team, which is set up suspiciously like a sanctuary. The Coach is giving a pre-race pep talk, much like a sermon. The racers should sit on or near their tricycles during the entire play. In the beginning the Coach should talk behind a pulpit; then he should come down to the racers' level for the rest of the play.

(**Director's Note:** The best arrangement is to make the set diagonal across the stage area. The Coach can almost have his back facing the audience during the pep talk, but he can turn so he is actually facing the audience somewhat. The racers can face him but also turn out a little so they are facing the audience, as well.)

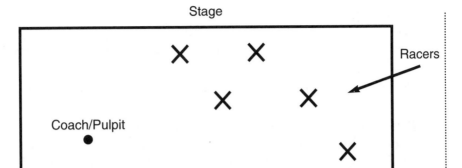

Stage

Racers

Coach/Pulpit

PROPS

Each character will need a tricycle. Only Marcus' trike needs to be in great shape. The second nicest one should go to Kyrie. The Coach should have a very worn trike to show the use over the years. Check the church nursery or ask church members with small children if you can borrow their children's trikes. No real uniforms are needed, but actors should wear similar types of athletic attire (shorts and T-shirts or sweats) to give the image of being racers. Each person should have a piece of cloth for polishing his or her trike.

The Coach also needs a whistle to hang on a string around his neck, a music stand or podium to stand behind while delivering his opening monologue, and a large-size book with the title *Tricycle-Racers Manual* on the front.

Other props include a small tool kit, a large towel (or something large enough to mostly conceal a tricycle), and swatches of construction paper (or cloth) for Marcus' proposed new handgrips.

THE SCRIPT
"The Heart of the Race"

(Lights come up dimly, leaving the stage only faintly lit; all the actors are frozen in place while the narrator speaks from offstage.)

Narrator: The Bible describes our life of faith in interesting word pictures. In Hebrews 12:1-2, Scripture compares the Christian life to being in a race. Ever wonder what it might be like if being a Christian were like being in a race you could see, feel, and hear? What if being a Christian meant joining a team in a...well, why not in a tricycle race? Let's use a little sanctified imagination to see what that might be like.

(Lights come up in full, and actors come to life. Coach is standing behind a music stand or podium, ready to deliver a "sermon." During the Coach's introductory sermon, racers periodically shout "amen" and "Preach it, Coach!" as if in a fiery, exciting, pre-race pep rally. For the duration of the play, each character should always stay near or on his or her tricycle—even when moving around the stage.)

Coach: *(Like an enthusiastic preacher)* I can see by your tricycles that all of you are ready to race! Now your tricycle is the very heart of the race—the vehicle that carries you through the course. In fact, if you have a trike even as small as a mustard seed, you can ride over mountains.

(Ooohs and aaahs from the racers.)

Coach: It's what gets you into the race, and it's what keeps you going to the finish line. But I must warn you that there will be rough spots along the way; the course won't always be smooth and straight. There will be sharp curves, uphill climbs, bumps, and detours. And the crowd won't always cheer you on. There may be hecklers along the way who want you to drop out. Sometimes you'll feel like the race isn't worth it, like you're ready to pull over and sit on the curb. When you start to feel like that, just open your *Tricycle-Racers Manual* to section 19, chapter 23.

"Yea, though the pavement is bumpy and the hills are steep, I shall keep pedaling and not give up. And though my tires be flat and my pedals be squeaky, I shall persevere and not fall off my trike, for the Racing Commissioner is with me."

I must also remind you that even though you're at different stages, you're all in the race together. No one is better than anyone else—even if you've been racing longer or if your tricycle seems shinier than someone else's. There's no prize for first place because everyone who finishes the race has the victory. Now, let's get ready to race!

Kristin: *(On her tricycle, as always, pumps pedal like a motorcycle clutch.)* All right! Let's go!

Kyrie: *(Sits on the edge of her trike, tentatively raising her hand.)* Um, Reverend Coach?

Coach: Yes, Kyrie, what is it?

Kyrie: *(Acts nervous, afraid to look at others.)* Well, you see, I'm kind of new at this, and, well, I was wondering if...oh, never mind.

Coach: *(Gets on trike and pedals over to her.)* Go ahead, what's your question?

Kyrie: Well, I guess I'm not sure exactly how to get started.

Kent: *(Lies on the floor on his back, with his feet propped on the handlebars.)* Oh come on. It's easy. Just read the manual.

Coach: *(Opening the* Tricycle-Racers Manual*)* That's a good idea. Let's turn to the second chapter and the 12th section. "As is a camel without humps, so is the racer who forgetteth his trike."

Kyrie: So I have to at least have a tricycle?

Coach: That's correct. That's the first step. And that is a nice trike you've got there, Kyrie.

Kent: How about chapter 3, section 29?

Coach: Excellent choice. That's one of my favorites. "Steep, steep are the hills of the course. Pedal steadfast and true, and the wind will caress your face on the way down."

Kent: And then there's . . .

Kyrie: Um, Reverend?

Coach: Yes?

Kyrie: (*Apologetically*) I've, um, read the manual, and I do have the trike, but I guess I still have some questions on how to actually get started.

Kristin: The best way to start is to just go! Now who's with me?

Marcus: Now wait a minute. For someone who's just started racing, that's a little hasty. You should make sure your tricycle is in good shape. The first thing I ever did was to polish it really well. You want to look good no matter how you ride. (*Pulls out cloth and starts polishing.*)

Kyrie: (*Doubtfully*) Yeah. I could polish it. That doesn't sound so hard.
   (*Notices Tyler who is trying to cover his tricycle with a towel.*)

Kyrie: Is that what you're doing, Tyler?

Tyler: (*Startled*) What? Oh, yeah, sure. (*Pretending he was going to use the towel to polish the trike*) Polishing is great. I think you could start that way.

Coach: Actually, if you ride a good race, your tricycle is going to get dirty. Let's not forget these are practical trikes designed to last a lifetime.

Kyrie: So appearance isn't as important as actually riding?

Coach: Exactly. To start the race you must get up on that trike and trust that the Racing Commissioner's signs will direct you the right way to go.

Kristin: So, Coach, let's get going!

Coach: Not too fast there; we're all in this race together.

Kyrie: We are?

Kent: (*Sneering*) You didn't think you'd have to race alone, did you?

Kyrie: (*Flustered*) Well, I didn't know, I mean . . .

Marcus: Well, some of us want to polish first, so give us a minute.

Coach: (*Trying to be diplomatic.*) OK, let's take a minute or so to polish.

Kent: (*Sits up and starts to polish, looks at Kristin.*) Yeah, and you can use the time to reflect on what polishing your trike means to you.

Kristin: (*Starts polishing.*) OK, OK. I'll polish, but then let's get going, OK?

Coach: All right! We have a plan. Feel better, Kyrie?

Kyrie: Yes. (*Polishing her own trike*) I think I'm getting the hang of this. So now we just jump on and go?

Kristin: (*Putting her cloth away and getting ready to ride*) That's the idea!

Marcus: (*Opening up his tool kit and tinkering with the trike*) Now hold on a minute! You should always check out your tricycle before you start to ride. Do all the parts work right?

Kyrie: I think so. I really don't know that much about my trike.

Kristin: (*Rides around in whatever area is available, even "through" others if there's room.*) What's not working could be fixed along the way.

Marcus: I think you're taking an awful risk if everything isn't checked out before you go.

Kristin: If you wait until you're completely prepared you'll never leave!

Coach: I think you're both right. You need to be prepared, but understand that at some point you have to hop on your tricycle and go.

Marcus: (*Proudly*) Well, mine is perfect. No troubles anywhere.

Kristin: So that's it then. We're out of here.

Marcus: (*Suddenly cautious*) No, I didn't say that. I need to check my rear wheels one more time. (*Gets off to have a look.*)

Kent: I think it's a good idea to know every detail of your tricycle. (*Looking directly at Kristin*) That way there'll be no surprises along the way.

Tyler: You know every part?

Kent: Every last one; they're all listed in the manual. Don't you know all the parts?

Tyler: Well, I've been meaning to get around to that.

Marcus: (*Annoyed*) Tyler, you don't know anything about the parts on your trike. You've had that broken spoke for weeks.

Tyler: (*Putting towel over the broken wheel*) I'll get around to it. I've been meaning to fix it. It's just . . .

Kent: You're afraid someone might see you in the parts store, aren't you?

Tyler: (*Defensively, starting to edge away from the trike a little*) Well, they might. You never know who you'll run into.

Kent: If you spent enough time in the manual you'd know the parts you need, and then you could order them by phone. No one has to see you.

Marcus: (*Helpfully*) Every Sunday morning they talk about tricycle racing and ordering parts on TV. You can order direct.

Kristin: Coach, do you really think it's necessary to know everything about your trike?

Coach: (*Pedaling over to Tyler and scooting him back toward his trike*) Well, it's a good idea to try. But what will really help is becoming familiar with the *Tricycle-Racers Manual*. It lays everything out for you. That way you always have the information you need when you get into a tough spot on the road. And besides that, it helps you understand the difficult parts because you're really taking the time to know what the Racing Commissioner has said.

Kent: I think it's best to memorize the manual.

Kyrie: (*Picking up the book the Coach left near her*) Memorize this whole thing? I don't think I could do that.

Kent: Sure you can. Just sit down and start at the beginning. That's how I did it.

Kyrie: You've memorized it all?

Kent: Well, actually I still have to finish the last chapter. Then I'll be done.

Kyrie: How long did it take you?

Kent: (*Nonchalantly*) About three years.

Marcus: (*Sarcastically*) I think it's more important to understand it than to just memorize it.

Kyrie: (*Putting the book down and turning away from it*) This is terrible! I didn't realize it took all of this just to be in the race.

Kristin: (*Riding over to her*) It doesn't! Coach, what about trusting the Commissioner?

Coach: Oh, that's true. It says in the Manual that you must have a tricycle to enter the race, but you must trust that the Commissioner will give you strength to last for the entire race.

Kyrie: (*Shuddering*) But what if you fall off the trike?

Coach: You brush yourself off and get back on. The trike is still ridable.

Kent: (*Patting his handlebars*) I'm not worried, not when I'm ridin' this baby.

Kyrie: But have you ever taken a spill?

Marcus: Of course he's fallen. I saw him dump it last week!

Kent: And you never have?

Marcus: (*Shrugging his shoulders nonchalantly*) Just once.

Kristin: That's because he never gets on it. He's always polishing his tricycle and tinkering with it and . . .

Marcus: (*Defensively*) You have to be prepared before you go pedaling off so fast. Kristin, you fall all the time.

Kristin: (*Equally defensive*) At least I'm moving toward the finish line!

Kent: (*Putting his tools away*) I'm not so sure moving counts.

Coach: Moving does count, because every time you get back on your tricycle and ride again, you are a wiser and more mature rider. More like the Racing Commissioner.

Kristin: (*To Kent*) So you think that knowing the manual is the most important thing—more important than actually racing?

Kent: Well, I . . .

Coach: The manual tells you all about how to race, but that doesn't change the fact that we all must be in the race and experience it for ourselves.

Kyrie: (*Trying to make peace*) You fall a lot, Kristin?

Kristin: I'm getting better at staying on. I fall off a lot less than I used to.

Kyrie: Doesn't that hurt?

Kristin: Sometimes. My pride, mostly, though.

Kyrie: But don't you ever think that maybe it's just not such a great trike?

Kristin: There's nothing wrong with the trike. It's usually because I'm going too fast or I get distracted or something. But I'm learning as I go.

Kyrie: What about you, Tyler? Do you ever fall?

Tyler: Well, I haven't really ridden that much. I mean, not in public, anyway.

Kyrie: Do you fall when you're by yourself?

Tyler: Well, there was this one time when I thought I would really get into the race, so I tied these pillows all over myself so that if I did fall I wouldn't get hurt.

Kyrie: And how did it go?

Tyler: Well, to tell the truth, uh... You see these friends came over, and they kind of laughed about the pillows, so I never actually tried it.

Kyrie: Have you ever tried pillows, Coach?

Coach: *(Riding back over to Kyrie)* No, but it's a good idea to surround yourself with mature racers who can encourage you and help you up when you fall off. Remember, we don't race alone. That's why there are so many racing clubs.

Kyrie: Who helped you start?

Coach: My parents taught me to race. I was very young, and my parents made sure I was always on carpet until I really understood how to ride. I was just a little guy, so I didn't have far to fall. Now I just take the scraped elbows and keep going.

Kristin: That's exactly what we should do. Get going!

Marcus: Don't be in such a hurry. To tell you the truth, I'm waiting for a new pair of handgrips.

Kristin: New handgrips? Why?

Marcus: I'm just not sure I'm happy with these. *(Holding up color swatches)* What do you think of this color?

Kristin: It doesn't matter what color they are as long as you can hold onto them!

Marcus: The color is very important—to me, anyway.

Kyrie: I think they're a nice color, Marcus. Do you think a new color will really help? Maybe I should switch colors.

Marcus: *(Handing swatches to Kyrie)* It's a matter of feeling really good about the way your trike looks. You wouldn't want to be embarrassed by it, would you? You never know who you're going to see while you're racing.

Coach: Personally, Marcus, I think you should be satisfied with your tricycle the way the Commissioner gave it to you. The color of your handgrips isn't really that important.

Kent: And besides, the manual doesn't ever mention the color of the handgrips.

Marcus: So you think I should buy a new color jacket instead?

Coach: It's good to think about how you're being perceived, but I think maybe we're off the point just a little bit. Kyrie, I don't think you need to worry about color coordination just yet.

Kyrie: *(Handing swatches back)* Oh.

Kent: *(Sarcastically)* Yeah, that's for the really mature racers.

Kristin: Can we please get going? The race is going to be over before we ever get started. Who's with me?

Kyrie: Wait. Can I ask just one more thing?

Coach: Of course.

Kyrie: How do you know if you're ready to be in the race? I mean, what if you have doubts?

Kent: That's easy! Just ask the Racing Commissioner.

Kristin: Hey, don't make it sound so simple. I've talked to him a lot, Kent. Sometimes I don't understand the things he tells me. Or even why he answers the way he does.

Coach: You just have to trust in his wisdom. After all, he wrote the *Tricycle-Racers Manual*. He knows how the race is going to go, he knows what will happen to your trike, he even knows when you'll fall off. The manual is written to anticipate all these difficulties.

Kyrie: This is all really confusing.

Coach: Some of the manual you actually won't understand until you're in the middle of the race—then the meaning becomes obvious.

Kristin: That's why I want to get going! It looks and feels quite a bit different out there in the race compared to sitting here talking! Let's hit the road, Jack!

Tyler: *(Sitting on the floor looking depressed)* All this talk reminds me that this race seems like so much work. You know, not many people are using tricycles these days. Maybe I should try a bike.

Kyrie: A bicycle. I never thought of that before!

Tyler: Sometimes I think I might switch over. A lot of people are bicycle racers.

Kyrie: Maybe that's what I should do.

Coach: No, Kyrie, you really don't want to do that.

Kyrie: But they're kind of the same thing, aren't they? Aren't they all in the same race?

Coach: No. They aren't in the same race. And they are very different. You see, a bicycle may look a lot like a trike, but it doesn't have that essential third wheel. That's what sets the tricycle apart. The differences are greater than the similarities.

Kyrie: How about a wagon, then? It's got four wheels!

Coach: It's very easy to be deceived by looks. But if you put your trust in the Racing Commissioner, you'll come to understand that the tricycle is the one true racing vehicle.

Kyrie: How do you know?

Coach: It hasn't failed me when I put it to the test in the daily races. You see, you could tip over on a bicycle. There's no stability. And a wagon, well, there's no power in it. You can't get anywhere—unless you find someone to pull you. And the Racing Commissioner says that others can help you, but they can't race for you.

Kent: (*Lying down and putting his feet up again*) Maybe if you have to ask all those questions, you're not ready to be in the race at all.

Marcus: Yeah. You really shouldn't talk like that. Someone might think you don't know what you're doing.

Kristin: But she doesn't! None of us really do. We're just doing our best and trying to get better.

Kyrie: (*Embarrassed*) I was just curious. I'm really so new to all of this.

Kristin: Come on, people. Let's go. We can talk about all these things on the way. The race has started!

Coach: This time I think Kristin's right. Everyone get ready.

(*Everyone except Kristin and the Coach hesitates.*)

Kristin: Come on. Who's going with us? Kent?

Kent: (*Getting up slowly*) Sure, why not. You might need some more advice along the way.

Kristin: Tyler?

Tyler: Um, I don't know. More and more people are riding mountain bikes. All those people can't be wrong.

Coach: Maybe if they knew more people were riding tricycles they'd want to ride them, too.

Tyler: (*Putting the towel over his trike and walking off stage*) I doubt it. They'd probably laugh or say something mean. I could lose a friend. No, I think I'll just go home.

Kristin: Come on, Marcus.

Marcus: (*Starting to polish again*) I'll be along soon. I really need to wait for those new handgrips. Don't worry. I'll bring up the rear later.

Coach: Will you come with us, Kyrie?

Kyrie: (*Hesitantly*) I'd like to.

Marcus: You still have some smudges on your trike. Why don't you wait with me. It'll give you time to finish the job.

Kristin: Don't worry about that; your trike will get plenty dirty during the race. Come with us, Kyrie.

Kyrie: But I don't understand everything in the manual.

Coach: You can test it out on the road. There's no better way.

Kyrie: You think I should go even though I'm not color-coordinated and I don't know all the parts?

Coach: Absolutely!

Kristin: And you don't have to worry. If you fall off, the Racing Commissioner is always nearby. And we'll be right there with you, too.

Kyrie: All right! Let's go! I've wanted to get in on this race for a long time.

Coach: Here we go!

(The Coach leads, then Kristin follows with Kyrie close behind and Kent in the back. They pedal into the congregation, down the aisle, and out the door.)

Kyrie: *(As she rides)* This is great!

Kristin: I told you it would be!

Coach: *(Before they leave the auditorium)* There's a sharp curve up ahead. Be careful!

(Lights fade halfway. Actors freeze on stage while the narrator speaks.)

Narrator: We may not ride tricycles in our Christian life, but as Hebrews 12:1 tells us, "We have around us many people whose lives tell us what faith means. So let us run the race that is before us and never give up. We should remove from our lives anything that would get in the way and the sin that so easily holds us back." May God grant good riding to us all!

THE END

GONNA MAKE YOU A STAR, JESUS, BABY!

BY RICH MELHEIM

....

*" 'If people want to follow me, they must give up
the things they want. They must be willing even to
give up their lives to follow me' "*
(MARK 8:34b).

THEME
Following Jesus.

SUMMARY
Flavius Maximus, Jerusalem talent scout and publicist, is in desperate need of a hot client in order to keep his business afloat. He sends an assistant to check out Jesus and report back with a transcript of the Sermon on the Mount. He concludes that Jesus' words need a rewrite or no one will ever follow him.

(**Director's Note:** The transcript of Jesus' speech that Flavius Maximus and the others read in this play is actually taken from Matthew 5, NKJV.)

CHARACTERS
Flavius Maximus–A slightly slimy talent agent, he is in need of a big client. His voice could sound suspiciously like television's Inspector Gadget.

Marge–Flavius Maximus' slightly sloppy office worker, she'd rather do her nails than answer the phone. Her voice has a nasal, singsong quality with a heavy Brooklyn accent.

Assistant–Flavius Maximus' assistant, who was sent to check out Jesus' potential for super stardom.

SETTING
An office.

PROPS
Desk, chair, two phones, bottle of nail polish, one card with a list of business titles on it, a red pen, and two scrolls (rolled-up paper will suffice). You'll also need appropriate stage lights and sound.

THE SCRIPT
"Gonna Make You a Star, Jesus, Baby!"

(Scene opens with a phone ringing. Lights come up on Marge doing her nails while ignoring the phone. Flavius Maximus, the proprietor of the talent agency, is pacing about.)

Flavius Maximus: Marge! The phone! *(Nervously looking at watch)* Where is he? Twenty minutes late. Twenty minutes! I don't have time for this. The speech has been over for at least an hour, and that lazy assistant of mine was supposed to get back to me with the transcript by now. If I don't land this new client—and soon—the whole company goes belly up! Marge, the phone! (*Looking at watch*) Twenty-one minutes now. Twenty-one minutes! Where is he? I'll read this speech in the history books before I ever get a copy. (*Angrily*) Marge!

(*Secretary scrambles to grab the phone while squinting at a card she lifts off the desk.*)

Marge: (*Using nasal tone and a singsong Brooklyn accent*) Let's see. Line three…line three. Oh, yeeeaaah. (*Pressing button*) Flavius Maximus Agency. No matter who you are, we'll make you a star. How may I help you? (*Listening*) Oooh. (*Surprised*) Oooh! (*Eyes wide and frightened*) Ooohhh! Better take this one yourself, Mr. Flabbiest.

Flavius Maximus: That's Flavius. Flavius Maximus.

Marge: (*Holding hand over phone*) It's one of your former clients. He says he's going to sue.

Flavius Maximus: Sue? Just what I need! Flavius Maximus here. (*Listening*) Julius, baby! What…(*Cringing*) yes, but…I know but we…I don't think you under…(*Holding phone away from ear as someone screams on the other end of the line*) But I booked your boy at the Coliseum, didn't I? Lions? Of course we knew about the lions. (*Whispering to Marge*) Did we know about the lions? (*To phone*) And gladiators? Hey, that's entertainment. (*Holding phone away as client screams again*) Look, tell you what. Bring your boy in, and I'll give him a free image-consultation make over. (*Listening*) What? OK. Bring whatever is left of him in.

(*Another line rings.*)

Marge: (*Squinting at card on desk before answering*) Let's see. Line one. Line one. Oh, yeeeaaah! Gluteus Maximus Literary Agency.

Flavius Maximus: That's Flavius. Flavius Maximus. Not Gluteus.

Marge: (*Covering receiver*) What's the difference? (*Into phone*) Gluteus Maximus Literary Agency. If writing fame's your goal, we'll get you on the scroll. How may I help you? (*Listening*) I'm sorry. He's on another line right now being sued.

Flavius Maximus: (*Waving at her*) I'll take it. (*To phone*) Sorry, Julius, baby, I've got another call. Ciao (*pronounced "chow"*) for now. (*Punching other line*) Flavius Maximus. What? Josephus, baby! How are…What? No. No, I don't think you have an ounce of talent, imagination, or originality in your body. (*Glancing around*) But that doesn't mean the ignorant masses won't love your writing. (*Listening*) What? She told you what?

Marge: (*Doing her nails again*) I told him the only way anybody's going to read his stuff is if he sticks the scrolls in clay pots, buries them in a cave down by the Dead Sea, and waits for some archaeologist to dig them up.

Flavius Maximus: No. No. She doesn't speak for the company. No. If I like it, if I like it, if I love it, I'll keep it. Yes. Send it over right now. *(Phone rings.)*

Marge: Line two. Line two. Let's see. *(Picking up card)* Oh, yeeeaaah! Flavius Maximus Concert Productions. If you sing way too loud, we can get you a crowd. How may I help you? *(To Flavius)* A Mr. Nero, sir.

Flavius Maximus: Nero? *(Rubbing his hands together)* Oh, he's big. He's big. Lousy musician, but big. Just what we need to inject a little cashola into the failing operation. A big, bad client. *(Punching in line)* Nero! Baby! What...yeah. Yeah, we've been in the business for eons. Our first client was Samson. Heard of him? Yeah, he really brought down the house. Heh, heh. What? Pyrotechnics? Of course we can handle concert pyrotechnics. Here's my idea: Instead of just lighting the stage, we'll light up the entire hillside for your fiddle concert. Sorry, violin concert. What do you think? *(Listening)* Safe? Of course it's safe. What—you think we'd burn down the whole town? Ha! *(Phone rings.)*

Marge: Line four. Line four. *(Squinting at card)* Oh yeeeaaah! *(Picking up phone)* Flavius Maximus Publicists, Image Consultants, and Star Makers. With a few of our classes, you'll appeal to the masses. How may I help you? *(Listening, then covering phone)* Code red! Code red, boss! Hot client alert. One Mr. Judas Iscariot on line four.

Flavius Maximus: *(Covering receiver)* Judas Iscariot? I don't know any...

Marge: He works for Jesus Christ.

Flavius Maximus: Jesus Christ?

Marge: Precisely!

Flavius Maximus: Look, Nero, baby...gotta go. Ciao for now. Oh, one more thing: Consider starting the concert with "Come On Baby Light My Fire." Ha! Ta ta. *(Punching line four)* Judas! Baby! How did your boy do on the hill? The mount, yeah, the mount. *(To Marge)* This Jesus guy a baseball player, too? *(To phone)* Oh, yes. J.I., may I call you J.I.? Yes, my assistant just brought in the transcript now. We'll take a look at it and get back to you with a few edits and adjustments, along with our standard contract. But before that we need a little more info on your boy. First, the name Jesus Christ: like it, like it, love it. Gotta keep it. Christ means Messiah you know. Good start. OK, where was he born? Where? Bethlehem? You might as well have said _____ *(name a small town in your area)*. No, let's say he was born in Rome or Athens. More credibility. What? City where King David was born? Oooh! Like it, like it, love it. Gotta keep it. Bethlehem it is! OK, father's occupation? *(Pause)* Creator and sustainer of the universe? Hard to beat that. Like it, like it, love it. Gotta keep it. Now, where'd he go to school? What? No formal education? We'll have to fudge a bit about that one.

Let's say he went to _____ (*name a college near you*). That'll impress 'em. OK, we'll take a look at the sermon on the hill and…what? Yeah, mount. Sermon on the mount and see what Mr. Christ's potential for the mass market is. Say, OK if I call him Jesus? If he's anywhere near as good as everybody says he is, we're all going to make a bundle of sheepskin off him. What? Making money isn't what ministry is about? Look, Judas baby, one of these days you and I are going to have to have a little talk.

Assistant: (*Rushing in*) Got it, F.M.

Flavius Maximus: (*Covering receiver*) Where've you been?

Assistant: Sorry, F.M. I got behind a slow camel. (*Lifts up his foot and looks under shoe.*)

Flavius Maximus: (*Glaring and unimpressed*) Funny. Now where is it?

Assistant: The sermon on the mount?

Flavius Maximus: No, the Galilean commodity exchange report! Of course, the sermon on the mount! Where's my transcript?

Assistant: (*Pulling out a scroll*) Right here, big guy. Just like you ordered. His first big speech to the masses.

Flavius Maximus: It took you long enough. (*Into receiver*) Judas, baby, gotta go for now. Let's do lunch on Thursday. Ciao! (*To assistant*) What, did you have to cut your own papyrus for the scroll? Give me that. (*Pulling the scroll open*) Let's see. OK. OK. "Blessed are the poor in spirit, for theirs is the kingdom of heaven." Like it, like it, love it. Gotta keep it. Give the ignorant masses some hope. (*Looking up*) It's that man-of-the-people approach. OK. Let's see what else. "Blessed are those who mourn, for they shall be comforted." That's good. Shows compassion. "Blessed are the meek…inherit the earth." That's OK. So far, so good. (*Frowning*) What's this? "Blessed are those who hunger and thirst for righteousness." Hmm…sounds a little too religious, don't you think? (*Takes a red pen out of his pocket and crosses out that portion of the transcript.*) Oh, well. "Blessed are the merciful…they shall obtain mercy." That's reasonable. "Pure in heart, they shall see God." Getting religious again. (*Looking to assistant*) I think we should delete all references to God. Might offend someone.

Assistant: I can fix it. (*Taking pen and marking manuscript*) See God? Just add one "o" and there you have it. "Blessed are the pure in heart, they shall see Good."

Flavius Maximus: Like it, like it, love it.

Marge and Assistant: Gotta keep it.

Flavius Maximus: OK. "Peacemakers shall be called children of God." (*Marking*) Children of Good. Easy enough.

Assistant: You're not going to like this next one, F.M.

Flavius Maximus: What do you mean?

Marge: (*Reading over shoulder*) "Blessed are those who are persecuted for righteousness sake, for theirs is the kingdom of heaven."

Flavius Maximus: Blessed? The persecuted? No one's going to buy it.

Marge: It does have a certain idealistic ring to it.

Flavius Maximus: (*Firmly*) No, no, no. Don't like it, don't like it, don't love it. Won't keep it! People have to be taught to fight for their own rights. Claw and scrape and scratch their way to the top. Deep-six that last line. People aren't going to follow this Messiah if they think it's going to cost them something.

Assistant: I don't think he's going to go for it.

Flavius Maximus: Look, if he wants THE Flavius Maximus as his PR man, he's going to have to learn to take some direction. I know what I'm doing.

Assistant: It gets worse.

Marge: (*Taking the transcript from Flavius; reading on*) "Blessed are you when they revile and persecute you and say all kinds of evil against you falsely for my sake."

Flavius Maximus: (*Shaking his head in disgust*) Ahh! Negative. Much too negative. People don't want to hear stuff like that. It's not positive thinking. It's not constructive. Give 'em what they want, I always say. (*Taking pen and marking manuscript*) Don't like it, don't like it, don't love it.

Marge and Assistant: Won't keep it!

Assistant: Read on. It gets worse.

Marge: (*Taking scroll*) OK. "Rejoice…great is your reward…for so they persecuted the prophets who were before you." Oooh, I see. He's drawing a parallel to the prophets.

Flavius Maximus: The old "parallel to the prophets routine," eh?

Assistant: Might work.

Flavius Maximus: I don't know. I think we'd want to eliminate all the negative images. It might play OK in Capernaum, but before he gets to Jerusalem, all these negatives have gotta go.

Assistant: Rough town, Jerusalem.

Flavius Maximus: Rough? They'll crucify him if he doesn't change his tune. OK, what else? (*Grabbing the paper from Marge*) "Salt of the earth." Good analogy. "But if salt loses its flavor…no longer good for anything except to be thrown out and trampled underfoot"? (*Throwing paper back to Marge and painfully rubbing temples*) Ooohh! This isn't looking good.

Assistant: It does sound a bit judgmental.

Flavius Maximus: I told Judas to get rid of all this judging business.

Assistant: Who does Jesus think he is? God?

Marge: The next analogy is pretty good.

Flavius Maximus: *(Reading over Marge's shoulder)* "Light of the world...city set on a hill...lamp under bushel...Let your light so shine before others"—that's good—"that they may see your good works..." Ouch! He was on a roll, but there's that "good works" theme again. I say we scrap any reference to good works. It makes people think that following this guy might actually change the way they live.

Marge: Well, F.M., he does suggest a certain lifestyle for those who want to follow him.

Flavius Maximus: *(Dramatically)* Ix-nay on the requirements. We lose too many followers if we make him too hard to follow.

Assistant: Then you're not going to like the bottom of the next paragraph.

Flavius Maximus: What? What... *(Looking down)* "Unless your righteousness exceeds...the Pharisees...by no means enter the kingdom of heaven!" *(Painfully)* Aaahhh! Where does he come up with this? Doesn't he know anything about human nature?

Assistant: Set your standards too high, and no one can relate to you.

Marge: I kind of like it when he insults the Pharisees.

Flavius Maximus: The Pharisees? They'll kill him at the polls.

Assistant: The next part gets impossible.

Flavius Maximus: *(Takes scroll and reads.)* "You have heard it said...'You shall not murder...' but I say to you that whoever is angry without a cause shall be in danger of judgment." *(Hand on his forehead)* Oy! What next? "And whoever says to his brother...'you fool!' shall be in danger of hell fire." *(Tossing transcript in Assistant's lap)* I can't read any more of this!

Assistant: There's more. "Whoever looks at a woman to lust for her has already committed adultery with her in his heart."

Flavius Maximus: There goes the prime time audience.

Marge: That takes care of you, too, F.M.!

Assistant: *(Reading)* "If your right eye causes you to sin, pluck it out!"

Marge: Eeeooow! Gross. I like it.

Assistant: "Whoever divorces his wife..." Hoo boy, he doesn't hold anything back, does he?

Marge: I was starting to like this guy until he mentioned divorce.

Assistant: *(Reading again)* "Do not swear at all..."

Flavius Maximus: Jumping Jehosaphat! He's going to alienate everyone on the face of the earth!

Assistant: "You have heard that it was said 'An eye for an eye'..."

Flavius Maximus: Now we're getting back to some common sense.

Assistant: "But I tell you...whoever slaps you on your right cheek, turn the other to him also."

Flavius Maximus: I don't want to hear any more.

Assistant: "Give to him who asks you..."

Marge: Flavius, I want a raise.

Flavius Maximus: I'm asking—no begging—you to stop.

Assistant: "Love your enemies...do good to those who hate you."

Flavius Maximus: Who's going to listen to this? Next thing, he's going to tell us to be...

Assistant: "Be perfect, just as your Father in heaven is perfect."

Flavius Maximus: (*Loudly*) Perfect! Aaarrrgggghhh! His first major speech and he's already managed to alienate everyone in the entire universe! Who in their right mind is ever going to follow this guy?

Marge: I kind of like him.

Assistant: I think that's what F.M. means.

Flavius Maximus: Doesn't he know what the public wants to hear? This is no way to get anyone on the political bandwagon! You gotta make promises. You gotta speak in generalities! You gotta kiss a few babies!

Assistant: He did do that baby-kissing thing.

Flavius Maximus: You gotta be who the crowd wants you to be. You gotta do what the public wants you to do. You gotta be...

Marge: Wishy-washy?

Flavius Maximus: (*Glaring*) Flexible! (*Spying another scroll*) Adaptable. What's that other scroll?

Assistant: Press release on upcoming speeches.

Flavius Maximus: Give me that! (*Taking scroll*) What's this? "Sell whatever you have and give to the poor"?

Marge: I like this man. I'm poor.

Flavius Maximus: Foolishness! (*Reading*) "Treasure in heaven"? Right, who's gonna buy that? "Easier for a camel to go through the eye of a needle than for a rich man to enter the kingdom of God"?

Marge: I really like this man.

Assistant: There go the lobbyists!

Flavius Maximus: "Willing even to give up their lives to follow me"?

Assistant: There goes everybody else!

Flavius Maximus: (*Handing scroll back, then sitting with head in hands, sobbing*) This isn't going to work. So much potential, but this isn't going to work.

Assistant: Do you think we ought to look for another client?

Flavius Maximus: (*Sob*) I could have rewritten history with this guy. But no!

Assistant: If he's not the one, shall we look for another?

Flavius Maximus: I don't know, kid. (*Sniff*) I don't know. But one thing's for sure. Nobody is ever going to follow this Jesus if he starts talking about giving up stuff—especially if he wants 'em to give up their lives. People want an easy road. A comfortable religion or life philosophy. This talk about sacrifice is the surest way to squelch any movement before it begins. No, this Jesus fellow has no future now. Not after this. (*Sob*) And I could have made him a star.

Assistant: Cheer up, boss. Maybe we can land another big client soon.

(*Marge hands Flavius Maximus a box of tissues.*)

Flavius Maximus: Not like this one. This kid had (*blowing his nose loudly*) potential. This kid had charisma. This kid had miracles! This kid had...

Marge: You pegged.

Flavius Maximus: We'll never, ever find anybody like him again. It's over.

(*Long pause followed by the phone ringing. Marge doesn't budge before 10th ring as Flavius Maximus scowls.*)

Assistant: We'd do best to hitch our wagon to someone with a little more political savvy and a little less...

Marge: (*Moving toward phone*) Honesty. Let's see... line five, line five... what's line five? (*Squinting at chart*) Oh, yeeaah! Gluteus Maximus...

Flavius Maximus: (*Sniff*) Flavius.

Marge: Talent Agency. (*Singsong, nasal tone*) Even if you're a jerk, we'll get you some work. How may I help you?

Flavius Maximus: (*Sniff*) We'll never find another one. Never.

Assistant: (*Trying to console*) There, there boss.

Marge: Yes, sir, he's right here.

Flavius Maximus: (*Sniff*) It's all over.

Marge: Line five, F.M. One Mr. Barabbas?

Flavius Maximus: It's no use. We'll never... (*Sniff*) never... (*Sniffing and looking up*) Barabbas? (*Sniff*) Barabbas! (*Changing immediately to his confident, power-hungry self*) Now there's a fellow with a movement that's likely to go somewhere! A year from now, a generation from now, this Jesus fellow will be long forgotten, but the name Barabbas will be etched into cathedrals and chanted out in hymns by children across the world... or my name isn't Gluteus Maximus!

Assistant: Flavius.

(*Lines one, two, and three all begin to ring. Lights begin to fade. If no lights, Flavius Maximus walks slowly offstage with the phone.*)

Flavius Maximus: Barabbas, baby! You've come to the right place. Yes, indeed. This is Flavius Maximus. THE Flavius Maximus. And what miracle might I do for you today? Rewrite the Roman calendar beginning with your year of birth? No problem! I was just about to do that for another client, but you've got much more potential. What was your birth year? I'll tell you what: I'll have my people call your people, and we can do lunch. When? The Ides of March? No can do. I'm having lunch with Caesar that day. Yeah. Where? Caesarea, of course. They've got a great Caesar salad there with...what? I'll have my people call your people on that. You don't have any people? No problem. I'll sell you some of my people. Like 'em, like 'em, love 'em, but don't gotta keep 'em. And another thing...

(Voice fades out, lights go black.)

THE END

A DICKENS OF A TIME

BY EVERETT C. TUSTIN

"Do not change yourselves to be like the people of this world, but be changed within by a new way of thinking. Then you will be able to decide what God wants for you; you will know what is good and pleasing to him and what is perfect"
(ROMANS 12:2).

THEME
Growing Up.

SUMMARY

In a "Dickens-ish" manner, an over-zealous fast-food restaurant worker learns how today's choices affect tomorrow.

CHARACTERS

Jeff–An over-zealous assistant manager at Burger Boy, he has lost touch with his friends and places an excessive amount of value on his position of authority. Money and career have become all-important to him. He wears some type of fast-food uniform in the opening scene, his pajamas and slippers in Scenes 2 and 3, and regular clothes in the final scene.

Garrett–Jeff's friend, he struggles through the changes he sees in Jeff. He wears a letter jacket, jeans, and a T-shirt.

Sarah–An employee at the Burger Boy, she also wears a fast-food uniform.

Stephanie–She is another Burger Boy employee, wearing a fast-food uniform.

Richie Maroney–"The Assistant Manager of Burger Boy Past," he wears a uniform and carries a notebook.

Angel 1–Dressed like Clint Eastwood in one of his westerns, he wears rugged-looking boots, hat, and poncho. He carries two stick-ponies (broom handles with toy pony heads on one end) inside his poncho, and chews a toothpick. He has a large (fake) moustache and sideburns. Spurs on boots are optional.

Angel 2– Dressed like a flight attendant, she is wearing a nice dress, white gloves, and maybe a matching cap. She carries a large purse containing many items to rummage through, including two videos. Also brings with her a bag of microwave popcorn.

    (**Director's Note:** For a smaller cast, have Garrett double as Angel 1 and Stephanie double as Angel 2.)

SETTING

The easiest way to set up all the scenes is to direct lighting to different areas of the stage with a spotlight.

Scene 1–A back room at the Burger Boy restaurant. Most of the set (as in all the scenes) can be imaginary. Need a table in the center and four chairs around it.

Scene 2–Starts in Jeff's bedroom. Jeff wears pajamas and slippers. A Scrooge-like nightcap would be great, if possible. The room has a bed, a table with a television on it, a videocassette recorder, and a rocking chair.

This scene moves to a blank area of the stage where all the action described by characters is imaginary, as though it takes place somewhere above the heads of the audience.

Scene 3–Back to Jeff's bedroom. Angel 2 already present.

Scene 4–The finale. Return to the back room at the Burger Boy.

PROPS

As already mentioned, lighting effects will be necessary to help in scene changes. You'll also need Western music; a tape of thunder noises; the items listed in each character's descriptions; calculator, receipts, and note pad; cloth to wipe table; french fries; motel front-desk bell; and any other personal items characters might carry such as coats, purses, hats, and so on.

THE SCRIPT
"A Dickens of a Time"

SCENE 1

(Lights come up on the back room at Burger Boy. Sarah and Stephanie are seated at a table eating some french fries. Garrett enters, singing with gusto.)

Garrett: Hold the mayonnaise, hold the liver, special orders we deliver, all we ask is that you shiver to Burger Boy!

(He waits for a response from the girls, but there is none. They just stare into space.)

Garrett: C'mon, girls, that was a fine solo. No applause?

(There is still no response from the others. He sits down.)

Garrett: What's the deal with you guys, did someone run over your hamster?

Sarah: Just drop it, Garrett. You know what's going on.

Stephanie: Right, just drop it, if you know what's good for you.

Garrett: What are you talking about, Steph? I have no idea what your problem is. *(Sarcastically)* Did Jeffrey the Burgermeister crash on you guys again for spending too much time on personal calls with *(stands and salutes)* "The Official Burger Boy Telephone."

Sarah: You really don't know what's going on, do you?

Garrett: *(Sitting)* No, I really don't.

Stephanie: Well, news flash, Garrett. Your friend Jeffrey won't let us off work tomorrow. That means we have to miss the graduation boat cruise that every other senior in the entire school is going on. We ALL have to be HERE from 9 to 5.

Garrett: Wait a minute, he wouldn't do that. I mean, he's graduating, too. He has kinda lost orbit since he became assistant manager, but I can't believe...

Stephanie: Shhh, here he comes.

(Jeff enters.)

Jeff: Hello, Garrett. Did you get a copy of next week's work schedule when you came in?

Garrett: No, I didn't.

Jeff: Well here you go. *(Handing Garrett a work schedule)* I gave you all more hours since school will be out. I knew that you'd all want the extra money. *(He looks to the group and then says with sarcasm.)* Oh, no need to thank me. *(Starts to walk away.)*

Garrett: *(Looking at schedule)* Jeff, you're not serious about this, are you?

Jeff: What do you mean, Garrett?

Garrett: I mean having us all work tomorrow during the cruise.

Jeff: Certainly.

Garrett: Have you lost it completely, Jeff? I mean, you only graduate from high school once. I'm not gonna miss that cruise just so the Burger Boy has an extra cook.

Jeff: *(Firmly)* You will if you want a summer job to help pay your expenses to college in the fall.

Garrett: *(Knocking on Jeff's forehead)* Jeff... Hello, pal, it's me, your friend Garrett. You remember me, don't you? I'm the guy who helped you get through sophomore English. The guy who set you up on your first date.

Jeff: *(All business)* The reality is that there is money to be made tomorrow, and if Burger Boy doesn't make it, it'll be the Hot-Dog Pound or Tammy's Twisty-Fry City. Remember, friend, it's the early bird that catches the worm.

Stephanie: You mean we have to start serving worm-burgers now? Ugh!

Garrett: I don't want to catch worms, Jeff; I want to go on that cruise. *(Pauses.)* You really don't care, do you? *(Giving up)* I don't know what planet you've moved to, but I hope they can clone you a friend. I think I was the last one you had here on earth, and it looks like you've just lost me.

Jeff: *(Patting Garrett on the shoulder)* I'm sure you don't mean that, Garrett. When you get that extra bonus in your next check you'll be singing a different tune.

Garrett: You don't get it, do you? I won't be here. This cruise may be the last time I see some friends who are graduating. Tonya's going to England for the summer, then she's off to Boston College. Darin and Donna are talking about getting married and moving to Indiana, and...

Jeff: *(Coolly)* Well, I guess we need another head cook then. When one reaches upper management like I have, one can't expect ALL employees to agree with every administrative decision.

Sarah: *(Seeing an opportunity to score points with Jeff)* Well, you know, Jeff, I for one agree wholeheartedly, and...

Garrett: *(Cutting her off)* Upper management? Oh grow up! You're acting like a snotty kid who makes everyone play the game his way because he owns the football. Jeff, you're the assistant manager at Burger Boy. You make a whopping 25 cents an hour more than I do. *(Sarcastically)* Hail to the chief.

Jeff: Actually, 27 cents more, but Mr. Marley says I have a great head for burgers and a real future in fast food. It won't be long until I'm night manager, and then... *(grandly)* who knows?

Garrett: *(Standing up, gathering his things)* Right, the heavens open up for night managers. Didn't you learn anything when we were kids? Jeff, some things are more important than money and jobs—like people! You can't just...

Jeff: *(Clears his throat to cut off Garrett, then speaks.)* Well, it's time to close up for the night. I know that I can't always be Mr. Popularity around here, but someone has to make the hard decisions. *(Pointing to Sarah and Stephanie)* I expect to see you and you tomorrow. Garrett, you can pick up your last check Monday morning. *(Jeff exits.)*

Sarah: *(Feeling a bit foolish about her brown-nosing to Jeff)* I'm sorry, Garrett. I should've threatened to walk out, too.

Garrett: I almost gave in, you know. He's right. I was planning on this job to help pay my college tuition in the fall. I was just about to skip the cruise and come in tomorrow, but the notion that he was "upper management"—I just couldn't stomach that.

Stephanie: Well, when you come in on Monday, don't tell us about what a great time you had on the cruise, OK?

Sarah: We better go, or Jeff will be after us again.

(All three get up to leave. As they push in their chairs, Sarah laughs out loud, and the other two look at her.)

Stephanie: What is it?

Sarah: *(Laughing and imitating Garrett)* You make a whopping 25 cents an hour more than I do. *(Back to her normal voice)* This from the guy who cooks because he can't make correct change.

(They all laugh out loud as they exit. Lights dim but stay on as Jeff enters. He walks around the table, wipes it with a cloth, and sits down with receipts and a calculator.)

Jeff: Let's see. Sarah's till... *(punching on calculator)* not bad. *(Writes down a figure on a note pad and continues.)* And Stephanie's till... *(punching on calculator again)* oh well... she'll do better when all this graduation stuff is behind her. Plus, she needs to push the Bonzoburgers more. That's the problem, she just doesn't . . .

Richie: (*Ghostly voice over sound system*) Jeffrey . . . Jeffrey the Burgermeister.

Jeff: (*Still looking at receipts*) Look, Garrett, if you want a second chance (*lifting his head and looking around the room*) I can probably . . . Garrett, Garrett, where are you?

Richie: Garrett's not here, Jeff. It's me, Richie . . .

    (*Jeff gets up from his seat and looks around more.*)

Richie: Richie Maroney . . .

Jeff: Richie Maroney? . . . Look, are you guys playing around at the drive-up window again. I told you to knock that off. (*Exits where the others did a few moments earlier, speaking offstage.*) Hey, is there anyone out there? Cut it out, you guys! (*Jeff re-enters.*)

Richie: I told you, it's me, Richie. Richie Maroney. I'm the (*with voice echoing*) "Assistant Manager of Burger Boy Past."

Jeff: What? Who is this really? Steph? Sarah? Garrett? You guys are really starting to make me angry. I'll fire you all if you don't quit messing around!

Richie: You're not listening, Jeff. I told you, my name is Richie Maroney. I was the very first assistant manager at the Burger Boy. Nearly 50 years ago today I received my promotion from head cook. I've been given permission to return and try to help you not make the mistakes I did. Those mistakes led to living a life of regret, my friend.

Jeff: Is this for real?

Richie: As sure as Bonzoburgers are two-for-one this week.

Jeff: (*Suspiciously*) Are you from the head office?

Richie: You might say that.

Jeff: Then let me see you. How come I can't see you?

Richie: It's not time yet, Jeff. You have one last chance to change your mind and follow a new path on your own. If you blow it, more drastic measures will have to be taken. (*Voice fades out.*) Goodbye, Burgermeister . . .

Jeff: Don't call me that! I hate it when they call me that. Hey wait, Richie . . . Richie? (*He walks around the room, looking all over.*) Richie? (*Finally walks back to the table, picks up his stuff, and starts to walk away. Then slowly comes back to peek very carefully under the table.*) Richie? (*Standing up again, he takes one last look around the room, then shakes his head.*) My stomach hurts. Maybe I should lay off the secret sauce a bit. (*He exits. Lights out.*)

SCENE 2

(*Lights come up on Jeff's bedroom. Jeff is making preparations as if getting ready for bed. Talking to himself as he goes, Jeff takes off slippers, pretends to dim the lights, then sits down on edge of the bed.*)

Jeff: Real jokers, those guys. Nothing better to do on a Friday night than imitate Richie Maroney From Burger Boy Past. *(Shakes head.)* Sounds like something out of a Dickens' book. *(He lies down on the pillow and begins to drift into sleep.)* If they could just push the Bonzoburgers more. Focus on *(yawning)* achieving their Burger Boy career goals... that kind of stuff...

    (Richie enters.)

Richie: Jeffrey... Jeffrey...

Jeff: *(Still half asleep)* Is that you, Mom? I don't have to go to school anymore... I can sleep in...

Richie: Jeffrey...

    (Jeff rolls over so he's facing away from Richie. Richie approaches and sits down on the bed.)

Richie: Jeffrey... you smell like a Bonzoburger. Wake it up, buddy! *(He pushes Jeff.)*

Jeff: *(Sits straight up and lurches back from Richie.)* Hey! Who are you? What are you doing here?

Richie: Richie Maroney. Get out of bed.

Jeff: What?

Richie: Am I moving too fast for you? You don't remember me? I told you I'd be back if you didn't show a change of heart, so here I am.

Jeff: Wait a minute, I'm supposed to believe that you are the Assistant Manager of Burger Boy Past?

Richie: Believe it or don't, it's up to you. The bottom line is, I'm here to help you. Now c'mon. We've got a lot of ground to cover tonight.

Jeff: This is nuts. Who are you really? Next thing you're going to tell me is that there will be three spirits visiting me tonight.

    (Richie opens up his notebook and starts looking through the pages.)

Jeff: One will be a roly-poly kinda guy with a big laugh. He'll be a lot of fun. The next will be...

Richie: *(Cutting in)* No, only two. And they're not spirits, they're angels. They get kind of annoyed when you call them spirits, so don't.

Jeff: Excuse me?

Richie: I said you only get two angels. At least that's what it says in the notes. *(Thinking out loud)* Usually we send three. I'm not sure why there's only two this time. Maybe demand is too high these days. Or it could be a cost-cutting measure. *(Shrugs.)* Anyway, just two. *(He looks at Jeff, then shakes his head and sighs.)* I hope that's enough.

Jeff: This is ridiculous. Let's say I do believe you are who you say you are. And even as we speak some goofy angel is on his way here on a flying carpet or whatever. Why me? I'm not a bad guy, and it's not even Christmas!

Richie: Listen, Jeff. The Christmas gig is for our most famous clients. That Dickens guy made sure of that. But we send angels to speak to people all the time—Thanksgiving, Easter, National Library Week, even graduation. So here I am. I was sent to warn you, but your heart hasn't changed since we last spoke at the Burger Boy.

Jeff: I still don't understand why you picked me. I'm not Scrooge, I'm not an old man. "Bah humbug" isn't even a part of my vocabulary.

Richie: Let's just call it a little bit of preventive medicine. The choices you've made recently aren't the best you could do. You've begun to love things instead of people.

Jeff: I'll have time for people later.

Richie: People like Garrett?

Jeff: How do you know about that?

Richie: Part of the job description. Don't you see, Jeff? The choices you're making today will affect your life tomorrow.

Jeff: Well, sacrifices have to be made in order to get ahead in life.

Richie: (*Menacingly*) Maybe I should see if I can find a third angel after all.

Jeff: (*Jumps back on the bed and holds the covers up to his chin.*) OK! OK! Don't blow a gasket or something. It was just an observation.

Richie: Expect the first angel sometime after Letterman and the second after "Late Night Videos." (*Dramatically*) And remember, Burgermeister, you still have time!

(*There is a thunder noise, lights go out, and Richie exits. There's a second explosion, and Angel 1 enters. He's seated in the rocking chair when lights slowly come back up.*)

Jeff: (*To himself*) This can't be happening to me. I'm a good guy, I go to church, I don't listen to heavy metal, I...(*He sees the angel.*) Who are you?

Angel 1: (*His hat is forward covering his face, he speaks in a harsh, gravelly voice without moving.*) Letterman is over, son.

Jeff: You're the one who Richie told me about. Hey, you're no roly-poly, fun guy. You look mean and nasty. Listen, buster, my mom's just in the next room, and she's gotta gun...I think...Forget that, I'm outta here.

(*He puts on his slippers and starts to move toward the doorway but stops when angel stands up. The angel tips up his hat and reaches under his poncho as if for a gun.*)

Angel 1: Go ahead, make my day.

Jeff: (*Nervously*) I'm sitting down now, look at me sit. I wouldn't think of going anywhere. (*Sits down on the bed.*)

Angel 1: (*Laughs out loud.*) I just love doing that Clint Eastwood bit.

Jeff: What's so funny? You mean you're not gonna shoot me or anything?

Angel 1: Shooting you would be rather counterproductive, don't you think? (*Gestures to his outfit.*) Say, how do you like this get up? The boots are a little tight, but I think everything else fits pretty well, don't you? (*Sees Jeff looking at him open-jawed.*)

Angel 1: Will you get off of that bed already? We've got places to go, people to see.

> (*Jeff warily walks over to the angel and with a trembling hand takes hold of his poncho and closes his eyes.*)

Angel 1: What are you doing?

Jeff: I'm taking hold of your coat. Isn't that how this works?

Angel 1: Get real, pal. We ride these. (*He takes out two stick-ponies from underneath his poncho and hands one to Jeff.*)

Jeff: You get real. I'm not riding that thing.

Angel 1: You know, I can get ugly if I have to. Ever hear of Sodom and Gomorrah? That deal with Lot's wife—I had a hand in that.

Jeff: (*Gets on pony.*) I'm ridin', man, I'm an urban cowboy. Where are we going, anyway?

Angel 1: Your pony will get you there, just hold on.

> (*Theme music from "Bonanza" or some other recognizable western, plays as Jeff and Angel 1 "ride" to the open area of the stage. Music fades after a moment.*)

Jeff: Where are we?

Angel 1: Look there. (*He points to imaginary scene above the area where audience is seated.*)

Jeff: I can't see anything. It's all misty. I don't know if I want to look, anyway. How 'bout I just get along little doggie and ride on home? (*He starts to turn away.*)

Angel 1: Watch. This is your chance to see and understand. Don't you get it? Graduation is an important time in a person's life. It marks a new chapter, a new direction. Decisions you make now will determine your future, your career, your friends, your values. Choose wisely now, and your future may be bright; choose poorly and . . . well . . .

Jeff: (*Excitedly*) Wait, I see something! It's . . . it's me and Garrett when we were kids. We're getting ready to play ball in the park. Look. (*Pointing*) He's a captain. He was always a captain.

Angel 1: Are you on his team? Where are you?

Jeff: Oh, I'm over there, under that tree, by myself. Nobody ever chose me for a team. (*Looking at the angel*) I wasn't that bad, just a little slow-footed. 'Course I had trouble with the passing, catching, and tackling stuff, too. But still, they could've given me a chance.

Angel 1: Hey, look! Garrett's calling you over. (*Jeff looks back to the scene.*) He's bringing you into the huddle. Now you're all lining up. Nobody is covering you. There you go, down the sidelines. Not quite as fast as Jerry Rice, but...

Jeff: Look, I'm open! I'm open in the end zone!

Angel 1: Garrett sees you... he's passing you the ball!

(Jeff mimes making the reception and all the action that corresponds with the angel's description.)

Angel 1: You caught it, you're jumping up and down! I think you're going to spike the ball... Was that a spike? I thought they were supposed to... oh well, never mind. The rest of the kids are mobbing you. That must have been a happy day.

Jeff: It was. One of my best. The following Sunday, Garrett told everybody at church how I won the game for us. Garrett and I were inseparable after that. I guess I forgot about it somehow. *(He looks back to the scene.)*

Angel 1: Please go on...

Jeff: *(Upset)* No. I don't want to. I want to go home. Is there anything else you have for me?

Angel 1: No, nothing else. Are you ready to ride? *(Jeff nods.)* Here we go.

(Western music starts again as lights go out. Angel 1 exits. Jeff and Angel 2 go to Jeff's room.)

SCENE 3

(Music fades and lights go up on Jeff's room. Angel 2 is already sitting in the room behind Jeff.)

Jeff: *(Making gestures as if whipping his horse)* Giddyap boy. C'mon, you doggies... *(Looking around as lights come up to full. Suddenly realizes he's back in his room and stops riding.)*

Angel 2: Wow... you really ride tall in the saddle, Jeffie!

Jeff: *(He quickly turns around to see Angel 2 and then speaks, somewhat embarrassed.)* Oh, excuse me. *(Goes back and sits on the edge of the bed.)*

(Angel 2 punches motel front-desk bell, then stands and walks over to where Jeff is, still facing audience though.)

Angel 2: *(She mimics all the gestures that a flight attendant would make as she shares this spiel with airline passengers.)* Please reach to the seat in front of you, take out the safety precaution guide, and read along with me. If at any time during this visitation we experience a change in cabin pressure, an oxygen mask will drop down from the ceiling. Take the mask in your hands and breathe normally until told to do otherwise. In case of a water landing, your seat cushion will serve as a flotation device. Our emergency exits are located two to the front, two to the side, and two to the rear. If you have any problems, please notify... me, I guess. *(She giggles.)*

Jeff: (*Big sigh*) Uh... where are we going now?

Angel 2: I was just teasing you. We're not going anywhere. We're going to stay right here.

Jeff: Then I don't have to sit through any scenes from my past?

Angel 2: Oh yes, we still have to do that "memories" thing, but these are more like memories from your future (*Dizzy smile*) Yeah, that's it. Let's see... (*She goes over to her purse and starts fishing through it.*) I've got it... just a moment... no, that's my coupon book... I knew I should have kept it in my hand... here we go... (*She pulls a video out of her purse and hands it to Jeff.*) We have it all on video.

Jeff: It says, "Anne of Green Gables."

Angel 2: (*She looks at it again.*) Oh, you're right. I have to return that by midnight. Did I remember to rewind?

Jeff: (*Looks at video.*) Yes.

Angel 2: Good. Here, give it back.

(*He gives the video to her. She puts it back in her purse and pulls out another.*)

Angel 2: This must be the one. (*Looking at the cover*) Yes, this is it, "Revenge of the Burgermeister". Are you ready? (*Reaches in her purse to pull out a bag of microwave popcorn.*) Want some popcorn?

Jeff: (*Shaking his head*) No, thanks.

Angel 2: Are you sure? It comes with secret sauce.

Jeff: No, I'll be fine.

Angel 2: Great, well here we go. (*She puts video into player.*)

Jeff: Of course you know my VCR is broken. The audio doesn't work.

Angel 2: (*Sigh*) This is probably going to be REALLY boring then.

Jeff: (*Upset*) Just play it, will you!

Angel 2: Don't get huffy with me, Mr. Assistant Manager. I wasn't kidding about the water landing. Video or no, you may be in for a turbulent flight if you don't watch it.

Jeff: Sorry.

Angel 2: (*Brightly*) Forgiven. (*Pushes buttons on the VCR, then steps back and watches screen.*) There we go. I'm gonna fast forward through some stuff. You've already seen the football thing... we can skip the Sunday school scene... whew, glad your mom got rid of that beehive hairdo... here we are.

Jeff: What's this? It looks like a party on a cruise ship. (*Incredulous*) This is tomorrow!

(*Looks at Angel 2, Angel nods her head.*)

Jeff: There's Stephanie and Sarah. And there goes Garrett. Oh I see, they're all signing yearbooks. That's most of my graduating class. Looks like they're having fun. I wish I could hear what they're saying.

Angel 2: Yeah. Say look, Sarah and Stephanie are playing with a doll.

Everyone else is laughing. Boy, are they cracking up or what? What's the big deal? Oh, look. The doll has a little hat and a uniform—what does it say on the front...the writing is too small, can you read it?

Jeff: (*Dejectedly*) It says "Burger Boy." We gave those dolls out as a promotion last month.

Angel 2: What?

Jeff: That's the assistant manager uniform. That's my uniform on the doll.

Angel 2: Oh, I see. Boy, they're really having a good time. I'm sure they meant you no harm.

Jeff: Right.

Angel 2: Look, the image is changing. Something else is coming on the screen. That's funny. I recognize this place.

Jeff: What is it?

Angel 2: It's the homeless shelter, downtown, but it looks a little different. A little more run-down or something. Hey, look at all the people coming in for the evening meal, coming down the food line. Have you ever been there? They do good work.

Jeff: No, I haven't, and I don't see what this has to do with...wait! (*Excitedly*) Stop the video! Rewind! A little more...there! Right there! Now let it run. I can't believe it!

Angel 2: What? What do you see?

Jeff: It's Garrett! (*Getting off the bed and pointing to the screen*) Right there, with the chef's hat on, all the way in the back. He's the cook. He looks older, maybe 35 or so, but I know that's him. Look at him smile! He must be really happy.

Angel 2: He really does look contented doesn't he. (*Frowning at video*) Oh, what's this?

Jeff: (*Sitting up quickly*) That's the Burger Boy.

Angel 2: It looks like nobody's there. Maybe the restaurant is closed.

Jeff: No, look. There's one light on in the back room. There I am! It's me counting the receipts. (*Pauses.*) All by myself. I don't look very happy, do I? I wonder...(*He leans forward looking at the screen, then slumps down.*) Yep, there it is. (*Dejectedly*) Pinned to my shirt, right there above the pocket. It says, "Night Manager." It looks like I'm getting ready to leave for home.

Angel 2: Hey, nice car you got. Mazdas are hot! Jeff...what's wrong? You got a nice car, probably a nice home. There's nothing wrong with being night manager at a fast-food place.

Jeff: I know. It's not that.

Angel 2: Then what?

Jeff: I just wasn't a happy person. There I was, all alone...

Angel 2: Sacrifices have to be made, don't they? If you want to get ahead in life, some decisions you make may be unpopular, isn't that right?

Jeff: Look, I never wanted...

(*Loud thunder noise booms, lights blink out quickly, and Angel 2 exits. Another loud explosion, and lights blink back on just as quickly. Jeff stands alone in the middle of his room.*)

Jeff: (*Dazed, looking around*) Oh, man. (*Looks at his watch.*) Yes! It's still today. There's still time. (*Kneels down at his bed, words seem to come with difficulty.*) Oh, Jesus... I'm sorry. I didn't see how all those little choices can make such a big difference. They seemed so insignificant. I spent so much time the past few years making the wrong choices; please help me make the right ones. Oh, I have a lot to do. Jesus, help me to start right away. Amen.

(*Lights fade on stage. Jeff exits.*)

SCENE 4

(*Lights come up on the back room at Burger Boy. Stephanie and Sarah are busy preparing to start their shifts. Garrett enters.*)

Stephanie: (*Surprised*) Garrett, what are you doing here?

Sarah: You're supposed to be on the senior cruise.

Garrett: (*Ashamed*) I couldn't do it. I went home and told my dad what happened. Boy, did I get a lecture. (*Mimicking his dad*) "Got to learn responsibility, son. How do you expect to pay for college? On your good looks? You know as well as I do that summer jobs are hard to come by in this town." What else could I do?

(*The others nod, and all three hang their heads dejectedly.*)

Stephanie: (*Looking at her watch*) Well, I wonder why Jeffrey hasn't come in with the morning speech yet. After all, he's the one who called and told us to show up early for a meeting.

(*Jeff enters.*)

Sarah: Speak of the devil.

Jeff: (*Overhearing Sarah's comment*) I prefer angels, myself. Good morning! Nice to have you back with us, Garrett. It seems like you never left.

Garrett: (*Deadpan*) I can't tell you how happy I am to be here.

Jeff: Yes... well (*he pauses, looking at each face before continuing*), after our conversation yesterday, a lot has happened in my life. It's difficult to explain everything. You'd probably think I was a little nuts even if I tried, so I won't. Let's just say I had a "Dickens" of a time sleeping last night. (*He chuckles.*)

(*The others look at each other and shake their heads.*)

Jeff: Anyway, in light of the very poor attitude you three have shown recently, I really feel I have no alternative but... (*he drags this out for effect*)... but to... GIVE YOU THE DAY OFF! (*He starts laughing, jumps up and down, spikes an imaginary football, and raises his arms up in *the air signaling a touchdown.)* Boy, you should have seen your faces! I had you guys going so bad! Oh, and I've talked the manager into giving raises to all of you.

   (All three just continue to stare at Jeff in disbelief.)

Garrett: Jeff, are you all right?

Jeff: *(More seriously)* I know this may be hard to believe, but a few "friends" gave me some advice last night about growing up. Fortunately, I still had time to make some changes and think through the choices I'm making today. I want things to be different between us, and I'm asking for your friendship and your forgiveness. I'm asking for a second chance...and...*(He looks at his watch.)* I'm asking for a ride to the pier so we can catch the boat before it leaves on the senior cruise! Anyone have room in their car?

Stephanie: You bet! We can all four ride together if you want.

Sarah: *(In a hurry and grabbing Stephanie by the arm)* We'll be back in a few minutes to pick you up, but we have to change first. C'mon, Steph, we don't have much time! See ya! *(Both girls race out of the room.)*

Jeff: *(Looking at Garrett)* Well?

Garrett: Well...*(He pauses, just looking at Jeff for a moment, then continues.)* It's nice to have you back. *(Shakes head.)* Last night must have been something.

Jeff: Let me tell you, I could write a book.

Garrett: Yeah? Well anyway, your timing was pretty good. This cruise is going to be something special. A lot of the people we see today we may never see again, at least until the class reunion, and then they may be totally different people.

Jeff: You're absolutely right. Let's go.

   (They both gather their things and start to walk out.)

Jeff: Wait! *(He runs over and jumps up on top of the table.)* And God bless us, everyone! *(He gets down and walks over to Garrett.)*

Garrett: What was that all about?

Jeff: *(Smiling and shrugging his shoulders)* For some reason, it just seemed appropriate.

   (Lights out.)

THE END

A CHANGE OF OWNERS

BY EVERETT C. TUSTIN

....

"If anyone belongs to Christ, there is a new creation.
The old things have gone; everything is made new!"
(2 CORINTHIANS 5:17).

THEME
New Life in Christ.

SUMMARY
A man's heart has a new owner when he gives his life to God.

CHARACTERS
Bernie's Self—Bernie is 43 years old and has kept his "Self" on the throne of his heart his whole life. That "Self" is represented by this character. Somewhat of a slob, he should be wearing a T-shirt that says Self.

Bud—He is a worker sent to clean up and do work on Bernie's heart to the specifications of the Holy Spirit. He carries window cleaner and a sponge mop; also wears surgical mask and rubber gloves.

Gene—Bud's accomplice and co-worker, he carries an electric saw, address book, and a New Owner's Certificate. He wears full carpenters belt, hard hat, and the like.

Holy Spirit—The new owner of Bernie's heart, he carries a briefcase containing blueprints (can be of anything) and a small box labeled "Odor Away"; sharply dressed in suit and tie; kind, but authoritative.

SETTING
The stage is set to represent Bernie Kropfeld's heart. Seated on a sofa and watching a small black-and-white television is the heart's previous owner, Bernie's Self. There should be doorways that may be imaginary, leading to other rooms or areas of the heart. This will make more sense as you read the script. One door should be the door to the outside, through which Bud, Gene, and the Holy Spirit will enter.

PROPS
The items listed in the character descriptions and setting, as well as a TV schedule guide, remote control for the television, snack food (such as potato chips, candy bars, and cookies), empty potato chip bags and snack candy wrappers, and a 2-liter bottle of soft drink. You'll need appropriate stage lights and sound.

THE SCRIPT
"A Change of Owners"
(Scene opens with Bernie's Self lying on the couch watching television, eating chips, and drinking a soft drink straight from the bottle.)

Bernie's Self: All right! Only 10 minutes until "The Young and the Wrestlers." That's my favorite show! (*Picks up TV schedule guide.*) Wow, special guest on the "Orca Whidbey Show" is Mr. Spock. The topic is "Children of Alien Beings in the New York City Public School System: What They Have for Lunch." What a great day of television! (*Bernie settles in and stuffs chips into his mouth.*)

(*Just then, Bud, Gene, and the Holy Spirit walk up to the door whistling "Battle Hymn of the Republic" or another familiar hymn. The Holy Spirit opens the door, and all three step into the living room.*)

Bernie's Self: (*Looks up from the couch, startled, and speaks through a mouthful of chips.*) Hey, what are you guys doin'?

Gene: Uh, let me see . . . (*Pulls out small address book.*) Is this Bernie Kropfeld's heart?

Bernie's Self: Yes, it is. (*Begins drinking from the bottle.*)

Gene: Hi, I'm Gene (*waving*) and according to this (*unwrapping a certificate of some sort*), Bernie's heart has a new owner.

Bernie's Self: (*He interrupts his drink and spews liquid out of his mouth—though careful not to get it on any of the others.*) What? Wait a minute. Let me see that.

(*Stands up as Gene hands certificate to him.*)

Bernie's Self: There must be some mistake. Nobody told me about this. Bernie's heart has had just one owner since he was born. I can't believe he'd sell out now. He's 43 years old. (*Hands certificate back.*)

Gene: Well, there don't seem to be any mistakes in the paperwork; it's all right here in the Lamb's Book of Life.

(*Holy Spirit begins to walk around the room, checking it out.*)

Bernie's Self: (*Nervously keeping an eye on the Holy Spirit*) Lamb's Book of Life? What's that? Some kind of health club or something? I mean he is out of shape. Maybe this new owner will get him on some kind of high-fiber program and get him doing a little exercise, too. Bernie thinks fingertip push-ups mean changing channels with his remote.

Bud: Oh, I'm sorry, (*apologetically*) it's nothing like that. No, the Lamb's Book of Life isn't really a club. It means his soul is headed for heaven when he passes on. You see, the new owner is Jesus. His Spirit has already begun the process of moving in.

Bernie's Self: Say what? (*He bursts out laughing.*) You mean like "The Bible-Jesus"? "The Solid Rock"? "Son of God" and all that?

Gene: Certainly.

Bernie's Self: (*With amazement*) Not in a million years can I believe it.

Gene: (*Aside to Bud*) Sounds like this may be a big job.

Bernie's Self: Who's this guy?

Gene: This is my co-worker, Bud. He mainly does cleanup work, a little sandblasting, and repainting if necessary.

Bernie's Self: Hey, how long do you guys plan on hanging around? 'Cause I hope you're not thinking of making a lot of noise or anything. Things have been nice and quiet here for a long time.

Gene: Why don't you tell 'im, Bud?

Bud: (*Putting a hand on Bernie's shoulder, friendly but firm*) We'll be here awhile, so you might want to get used to it.

Gene: You see, as long as Jesus owns a heart he's always at work in it, making more rooms for carrying others' problems and sensitivities, tearing down walls of complacency, and installing carpets of compassion. You get the idea.

Bud: That's right, and it's great to see that work continue.

Gene: Well, Bud, I've got work to do upstairs. I'll see ya later, OK? (*Exits. From then on audience hears periodic electric-saw noise offstage throughout play.*)

Bud: (*Ignoring Bernie's Self*) See ya, Gene. Whew (*to Holy Spirit*), looks like this room is as good a place as any to start. (*To Bernie's Self*) I may be down here awhile. (*Unplugs TV, wraps cord around it, and sets it by the door.*) Adios, amigo. Sorry, sir, this just won't be needed anymore. (*Sighs.*) So much to do and so little time. (*Gets out spray bottle and starts squirting and wiping everything, even Bernie's Self.*)

Bernie's Self: Watch out!

    (*Holy Spirit ambles over to continue the conversation. Bud silently continues to clean area while Holy Spirit and Bernie's Self talk.*)

Holy Spirit: Good day! How are things?

Bernie's Self: (*Rather confused, looking around the room and at Bud cleaning*) Well, I'm not sure. You guys sorta walked right in, said you had a certificate for a new owner, then your friends just took off cleaning.

    (*Bud moves empty potato chip bags and snack wrappers off of the couch*)

Bernie's Self: Hey, I wanted those there! (*Suddenly suspicious, back to Holy Spirit*) Who are you?

Holy Spirit: Oh, excuse me, I'm the new owner. (*Shakes hands with Bernie.*)

Bud: (*Looking up from cleaning, sighs*) Oh, thank heaven!

Holy Spirit: Exactly. Bud, why don't you leave us for a while?

Bud: Certainly, sir. I'll go see if I can give Gene a hand upstairs. (*Picks up things, then exits to join Gene.*)

Holy Spirit: Be careful, nobody's been up there for quite some time.

(*Looking at Bernie's Self who kind of shrugs and avoids eye contact*) You never know what evil lurks in the hearts of men.

Bernie's Self: (*Dramatically*) The shadow knows!

Holy Spirit: Well, I do too, actually. Excuse me, would you have a seat? I'd like to explain . . .

Bernie's Self: It's about time. It's like I'm not even king of my own castle anymore!

Holy Spirit: That's the point.

Bernie's Self: What's the point?

Holy Spirit: You're not king.

Bernie's Self: What?

Holy Spirit: Of your castle.

Bernie's Self: What castle?

Holy Spirit: Well, actually it's my castle . . . better yet, temple.

Bernie's Self: Temple, castle . . . what are you talking about?

Holy Spirit: Let me show you. (*Holy Spirit opens briefcase and unveils blueprints.*) You see this? (*Spreads blueprints out on table.*) These are some of the plans we've made for this place.

Bernie's Self: We've made?

Holy Spirit: Bernie and I.

Bernie's Self: (*Sighs.*) I'm his Self, but I'm always the last to know! Nobody ever tells me anything! (*Looking at plans*) Hey, this looks nice. It's so big. It'll be great for parties. There are rooms here that don't even exist.

Holy Spirit: Not yet.

Bernie's Self: You mean you're gonna add on?

Holy Spirit: Of course. We need to extend the area of compassion. It was hardly big enough for anyone but Bernie. We need much more space for others. And then . . .

Bernie's Self: (*Cutting him off*) Wait, did Bernie sign this? This doesn't sound like him at all. He was perfectly satisfied with . . .

Holy Spirit: (*Cutting off Bernie's Self*) Oh, we've eliminated rooms for complacency if you look right here . . . (*Points on blueprint.*)

Bernie's Self: What? That was my favorite room. A guy could walk in there, turn on "Wheel of Fortune," and forget about everything. Nice music, too. The kind like you hear in elevators. You know, a place to get away from those nasty headlines, gave you a sense of . . . of . . .

Holy Spirit: Apathy?

Bernie's Self: Yeah . . . I mean no! Hey, we sent $5 to the Save the Whales campaign once. Don't tell me we don't care.

Holy Spirit: Uh . . . right. Well, we still feel a great need to expand the room for compassion and eliminate complacency. Here, let me show you a few more changes we have in mind.

(*They walk over to an area in the room and stand in front of an imaginary doorway.*)

Bernie's Self: The study? What do you want in here?

Holy Spirit: Well, to begin with it needs to be used.

Bernie's Self: Yeah, I know what you mean. It's been kinda vacant since college, hasn't it? Hey (*excitedly*), how about a big screen TV over there? (*Pointing*) This is the only room without a television, and I don't like it that way; I need something to keep my mind active.

Holy Spirit: Is that so?

Bernie's Self: Yeah, you know, game shows, soaps, cartoons. Nothing like a good game show to get the wheels spinning. (*Imitating a contestant*) I'll take Batman characters for $50, Alex. Ever watch that "Jeopardy" show? Man, I know that stuff. And soaps—the drama, the suspense...like sand through your fingers...so are the days of our livery stable.

Holy Spirit: I'm sorry, that's not what we had in mind. We'll be filling this room with reading material for the spirit.

Bernie's Self: I get it, soul food, right?! Ha ha ha...you get it, "soul food"?

Holy Spirit: Uh...yes, I'm afraid I do...very clever. If I may continue?

Bernie's Self: (*Still pleased with his little joke*) By all means.

Holy Spirit: Thank you. Picture book...

Bernie's Self: (*Excitedly*) Picture books? I like those!

Holy Spirit: (*Firmly*) Let me finish, please. Not "picture books." Rather, picture bookshelves filled with the writings of the great ones, Bunyan, Bonhoeffer, Tozer, Augustine...

Bernie's Self: (*Frowning*) Bunyan? You mean like Paul Bunyan? Hey, I don't mind a little reading material, but how about names like Sidney Sheldon or something they could make a good miniseries out of? (*Getting excited again*) Ooh! Picture this: A video library of every episode in the "Star Trek" series. That would be great!

Holy Spirit: I don't think you've got the idea. This is meant to be a room of quiet. A place of prayer and meditation on God's Word. Bernie needs a place of solitude where he can hear "the still small voice" speak to him.

Bernie's Self: Still small voice? You mean like Jiminy Cricket?

Holy Spirit: I'm afraid we better move on.

Bernie's Self: Yeah, let's move on. If there's not going to be a TV, I won't hang around here much anyway.

Holy Spirit: (*Moving to the place where Bud and Gene exited.*) Is this the upstairs?

Bernie's Self: (*Fidgeting*) Uh...yeah but...

(*Bud and Gene shout from offstage.*)

Bud: Watch out!

Gene: What is that? Run, run!

(*Bud and Gene come bursting through the doorway. If using a real door, have Bud and Gene slam it shut behind them.*)

Holy Spirit: Hey… (*calming them down*) hey, what's going on?

(*Both talk at once trying to describe some big, hairy, ugly beast. Dialogue moves quickly back and forth between both characters.*)

Bud: (*Breathing hard*) It was big and hairy!

Gene: (*Cutting in*) About this tall (*making gesture with hand*) and bad breath! (*Pauses to catch his breath.*)

Bud: I've never seen anything like it!

Bud and Gene: And did it ever stink!

Holy Spirit: (*Cutting both of them off*) Wait a minute, will you please? One at a time!

Gene: I… (*panting*) I was walking around up there, mainly doing some work on the bedroom when I started to smell a funny odor. I went out of the bedroom and down the hall trying to figure out what it was. Well I opened the hall closet, and I tell you, the smell about knocked me over.

(*They all look at Bernie's Self who sheepishly tries to cover his embarrassment.*)

Holy Spirit: Go on.

Gene: Well, I figured whatever it was, it was gonna take some heavy cleaning before I could even begin work. Besides, it was all dark in there, too. Must be some kind of electrical problem. So I call Bud over and he starts hooking up the sandblaster, when all of a sudden…

Bud: (*Cuts in.*) All of a sudden this big, hairy, yellow-eyed thing comes chasing after me. I mean, talk about llama breath. That thing must have been hiding in there for years.

Holy Spirit: (*Looking at Bernie's Self*) About 43 I suspect.

Bud: We fended him off for a while with the glass cleaner, but he kept charging. It was just too much. Then Gene grabbed the Mop & Glo, you know, the industrial strength, and was after the beast in a flash, waving the sponge mop in its face like Zorro. But we still couldn't hold that thing off. It was all we could do to beat it down the stairs and get through the door.

Holy Spirit: Just as I suspected. (*Looking directly at Bernie's Self*) That closet is full of rebellion, isn't it?

Bernie's Self: Well, I wouldn't say full.

Holy Spirit: (*Pressing*) Isn't it?

Bernie's Self: (*Smiling sheepishly*) I guess there are some skeletons in everyone's closet, right?

Gene: Skeletons we can handle. This thing had meat on it.

Holy Spirit: Well, why don't you try this? (*Pulls an object from his briefcase.*)

Bud: (*Reading the label*) "Odor Away," it kills and deodorizes. Takes care of rebellion, all forms, also works on fleas, ticks, and roaches. *(To Holy Spirit)* Thanks, sir, we SHALL return.

(Both Bud and Gene exit through door.)

Holy Spirit: Well now, a few surprises. *(Speaking to Bernie's Self)* I figured we wouldn't have that kind of trouble here anymore.

Bernie's Self: *(Smiling)* Just keeping you on your toes.

Holy Spirit: Yes. Well, speaking of the bedroom, would you care to see what we've got planned for that room?

Bernie's Self: You're not taking down any of my paintings, are you?

Holy Spirit: Paintings? *(Looking at blueprints)* Let me see...you mean... *(Looks at Bernie's Self with disgust.)*

Bernie's Self: *(Defensively)* That's art. Culture.

Holy Spirit: That's pornography.

Bernie's Self: Beauty is in the eye of the beholder.

Holy Spirit: Love may be blind, but lust has 20/20 vision. That room is to be so pure that Bernie would never feel ashamed to show it to his Lord. Besides, one day he may be married.

Bernie's Self: Bernie? *(Laughing)* No way. Too many bad habits.

Holy Spirit: Habits he'll be breaking.

Bernie's Self: We'll see. It's gonna take more than Mop & Glo to clean up this heart.

Holy Spirit: This is true. Regardless, the bedroom will be a place of purity and sanctity when we've finished our work.

Bernie's Self: Well fine, all that leaves me is the living room. I can survive here. Just give me back my TV, a few bags of chips, and my remote control. I'll make do.

Holy Spirit: I'm sorry, I can't do that. This room is to be redone, also.

Bernie's Self: What? *(Melodramatically)* Is there no end to this torment? Are there no final frontiers for a real man's man?

Holy Spirit: The living room is for conversation with friends. Bernie may have others over to share in the Word, to encourage and affirm one another. We may leave the television, but *(pointing to imaginary poster on wall)* other things will have to go.

Bernie's Self: *(In disbelief)* Not my Woodstock poster. Look. *(Moving closer)* See right there, next to that guy in the Daktari hat?

Holy Spirit: Yes, I see...it looks like he has a hat on, too!

Bernie's Self: *(Triumphantly)* Yeah...that's Bernie.

Holy Spirit: What kind of hat is that?

Bernie's Self: Oh that's not a hat. Bernie used to have a lot of hair. It was wild! *(Gestures hair size with hands.)*

Holy Spirit: I'll say.

Bernie's Self: *(Nostalgically)* During the concert a pair of swallows built a nest in it...

(*Holy Spirit grimaces.*)

Bernie's Self: Such a beautiful moment. (*Noticing the Holy Spirit*) I guess you had to be there.

Holy Spirit: Apparently. (*Sighs.*) We'll be replacing that poster with a framed rendering of 1 Corinthians 13... "the love chapter." Yes, that will look nice.

Bernie's Self: You're kidding. Where am I supposed to stay? There won't be a room in this heart that I feel comfortable in.

Holy Spirit: Let me show you something. (*He picks up blueprints again.*)

Bernie's Self: What's that? It looks like a castle.

Holy Spirit: A temple. It's what Bernie's heart will look like when I'm done.

Bernie's Self: No way!

Holy Spirit: Well, that's the plan. Of course it'll take some time. And we can only do as much work as Bernie allows, but I'm confident that when he sees how positive the changes are, he'll give us free rein.

Bernie's Self: It looks great. But I don't think I fit in there anywhere.

Holy Spirit: (*In a comforting tone*) I realize these changes make you uncomfortable. But you see, Bernie wants to take his "Self" off the throne, and that's you. He wants to give Jesus total control of his life.

Bernie's Self: You mean that's it? I'm just out on the streets? (*Pleadingly*) Can I at least come and visit on weekends? Holidays? Super Bowl Sunday?

Holy Spirit: Well, there is another way.

Bernie's Self: (*Excitedly*) What is it? I'll do anything. I mean, well, I hate to admit it, but the plans you've made are pretty exciting. I'd really like to see the changes you've been talking about.

Holy Spirit: There are lots of hearts that have experienced a change of owners. Sometimes the transition is very smooth, sometimes it's a rocky road. The key is your attitude. (*Pointing to Bernie's Self*) It's difficult for someone who's been in charge for as long as you have to allow someone else to lead. In fact, if you walk through that gateway and take a good look around, you may see battles in many hearts over who will lead and who will follow.

Bernie's Self: So, what are you saying?

Holy Spirit: Can you become a servant?

Bernie's Self: (*As if he'd never thought of it before*) I think so.

Holy Spirit: Can you take instruction instead of giving orders?

Bernie's Self: Um... yes.

Holy Spirit: Will you think more about others and less about your own wants and desires?

Bernie's Self: (*Gaining confidence*) You can count on me. I think. I mean, I'll sure try.

Holy Spirit: Well, that's what we need. (*Glancing at the clothes Bernie's Self is wearing*) Your wardrobe could stand a little changing as well, but that can come later. Your attitude sounds good.

Bernie's Self: (*Excitedly*) Then I can stay?

Holy Spirit: Certainly—as God's servant. Now, why don't you go see if Bud and Gene can use some help? They'll be heading for the basement next.

Bernie's Self: (*Showing a look of fear*) The basement? Did you say the basement?

Holy Spirit: Yes.

Bernie's Self: I better hurry.

Holy Spirit: What's wrong?

Bernie's Self: I don't really want to talk about it right now if you don't mind. (*Bernie's Self rushes to doorway where Bud and Gene have been working.*) Truth is, I'm not sure what they'll find in the basement, but it might have teeth!

(*Holy Spirit shakes his head as he puts blueprints back in briefcase and Bernie's Self disappears through the doorway.*)

THE END

DEBTORS PRISON

BY PAUL NEALE LESSARD

....

*"He saved us because of his mercy. It was not because of
good deeds we did"*
(TITUS 3:5a).

THEME
Easter/Freedom From Sin.

SUMMARY
Three men are in debtors prison. In three scenes we hear their stories and come to an understanding of our own positions as debtors before God.

CHARACTERS
Duncan–A longtime resident of the prison, he is hard and gruff, aloof, always cool and unflustered.

William–Another longtime resident, he shows more emotion and is somewhat softer than Duncan.

Terry–A newcomer to the prison.

Prison Guard

Narrator–Person offstage who introduces the scenes.

(**Director's Note:** This play could be done with a female cast. Duncan would become Margaret Duncan, William becomes Mary, and Terry becomes Terri. Be sure to make appropriate gender-reference changes to the script when necessary.)

SETTING
A prison cell. One-inch dowels of varying lengths, painted black, and nailed to a 2×6-inch board placed across the front of the stage (downstage right and left) will serve as a grim reminder of the location. Downstage center is where the bench should sit. A table and two chairs are set stage right and a bunk bed is set at an angle, opening up to the audience, just to the left of center stage.

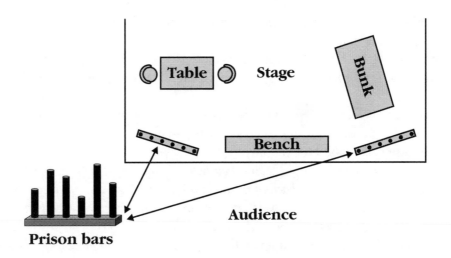

PROPS

A cassette or CD of blues music; a Checkers game; a few blankets (gray or tattered); a table and two chairs; a book or two for the table; a bunk bed (camp-style, angle iron would look the best); a narrow bench with no back (like a picnic-table bench); and soiled, dirty rags to use as handkerchiefs. The characters' clothing should be in neutral colors, drab and worn. You'll need appropriate stage lights and sound.

THE SCRIPT
"Debtors Prison"

SCENE 1

(As the audience arrives, have a cassette of blues-type music playing in the background. Reserve a seat in the middle of the auditorium for Terry. When it's time for the show to begin, fade out the music and bring up the lights on Duncan and William playing Checkers. Terry enters, wearing drab, tattered clothing and carrying a rolled-up blanket, and sits in the reserved seat.)

Narrator: *(Offstage)* In mid-18th century England, Europe, and even in Colonial America, it was not uncommon for men to be imprisoned with no hope of release as a result of bad debts. To be consigned to a debtors prison, as it was called, was to be forever condemned.

William: *(Sits up suddenly and moves a checker, jumping three of his opponent's checkers.)* Ha! King me!

Duncan: *(Waving his fist in William's face)* I'll king you all right.

William: *(Pointing at the board)* C'mon Duncan, king me. I didn't even cheat this time.

Duncan: *(Disgusted)* After all these games, you finally admit you cheat?

William: *(Ignoring Duncan's comment)* Right here, make this checker a king.

Duncan: *(Reluctantly crowning the checker)* Just because you're getting the first king doesn't mean you've won the game.

William: *(Gleefully)* Not yet, anyway!

(They continue to play, absorbed in the game. At this point the Prison Guard enters from the back of the auditorium carrying a dirty piece of paper. It has a list of names with descriptions on it. He stops about halfway up, looks around, spots Terry, and comes to the end of Terry's row. He looks back at his paper and then up at Terry, points to him, and motions for him to come. Terry slowly stands up, looks helplessly around, and points to his

chest. The Prison Guard nods. Terry, looking defeated, makes his way to the guard, who then escorts him to the stage. No words are exchanged. Escorted by the guard, Terry enters stage right behind the table. The guard then leaves. Terry looks at the two men, who seem oblivious to his presence, and then crosses to the bottom bunk to put his blanket there.)

Duncan: *(Without looking up)* I wouldn't put anything there if I were you.

(Terry stops, straightens up, and reaches to put the blanket on the top bunk.)

William: *(Clears his throat.)* Ahem...

(Terry stops once again and turns around to face the men, who still don't look up.)

Duncan: *(As he moves a checker)* I should think this one can sleep on the bench. What do you think, William?

William: Suits me fine. Under the window, maybe?

Duncan: *(With an air of finality)* Under the window on the bench.

William: It's best really; the last chap didn't last too long sleeping on the floor.

(Terry slowly crosses and places his blanket on the bench. He takes off his jacket and puts it on top of his blanket.)

Terry: It doesn't much matter where I sleep. I won't be here long.

William: *(With mock amazement)* Won't be here long? *(They both turn to look at Terry.)* Don't you know where you are, boy?

Terry: Sure I do; I'm not a fool.

Duncan: *(Back to his Checkers game.)* Then don't talk like one.

William: This is the Dunsmire Debtors Prison.

Duncan and William: *(In unison)* No one ever leaves.

Terry: No one?

Duncan: *(Contemplating his next move)* At least not alive.

Terry: *(Disbelieving)* What? Are you telling me that no one ever pays off their debts?

Duncan: *(Looking at Terry)* If you couldn't take care of your debts on the outside, what makes you think you'll be able to do it in here?

Terry: The jailer said that I could work off my debt.

Duncan: Don't build your hopes on a jailer's empty promise.

William: From our first day, we both tried to work our way out of this prison. It makes the most sense at the start. But after a while you come to realize that you owe so much and you earn so little.

Duncan: *(Back to his Checkers, shaking his head)* I'm surrounded by naive fools.

Terry: But my family! I have to get out. My wife and children cannot live with my brother the rest of their lives. *(Pause)* All it took was two bad crop years, and I was unable to pay the rent on the land we farmed. We had nothing to eat; how could they expect me to pay any rent? If only he could've given me another chance. (*Turning away*) I'm not a bad person.

Duncan: (*Sharply*) None of us is. It's just not enough to be good. You didn't measure up financially. None of us did, or we wouldn't be here.

William: (*Wishfully, playing an invisible violin*) I had a music shop. Violins, violas, cellos, and double basses. (*Looking at his hands*) I made instruments that brought music to the whole of England. And Duncan, well, he was a baker. His pastries, buns, and sweetmeats were the talk of Surrey. What did you call your bakery, Duncan?

Duncan: Duncan's Doughnuts.

William: He was famous even in London, where I lived.

Terry: I'm a farmer. Or was…

William: Well, you can learn another trade here. Like making shoes,

Duncan: or saddles,

William: or baking,

Duncan: or games of Checkers,

William: or license plates.

Duncan and Terry: License plates?

William: It's experimental. No one really knows what they're for. (*Shrugs.*) But, same as you, we fell upon hard times and were unable to pay our creditors, so we ended up in here.

Terry: (*Kneels beside his blanket and begins to arrange it like a bed on the bench.*) Well, I'll not be in here long. If I work hard and long enough, I know I can pay off my debts and get out of here!

William: (*Nodding his head slowly*) I wish it were true.

(*Silence as Terry arranges his bed.*)

Duncan: (*Jumping two checkers*) King me. It's your turn, William, but I believe the game may be mine this time.

William: (*Turning back to the game*) Maybe, but I'm still ahead of you 2,346 games to 1,998.

Duncan: So you've had a couple of good years. I've got plenty of time to catch up.

(*Fade to black. Fade in blues music while stage is dark. Fade out blues as lights come up for Scene 2.*)

SCENE 2

Narrator: (*Offstage*) Terry committed himself to working hard. It was not uncommon for him to put in 15- or 16-hour days, seven days a week in his efforts to pay off the debt that led to his imprisonment. Finally, after his first full year in the Dunsmire Debtors Prison, he asked the jailer for a review of his work. Terry wanted to know how far along he was in paying off his debt.

(Scene opens with Duncan and William playing Checkers again. However, William is lying on the top bunk, with his hand under his head, looking at the ceiling and humming. Duncan is engrossed in the game. He has only one red checker left, and the black checkers are doubled—all William's pieces are kings. Duncan is making blowing noises in his frustration as he tries to figure out his next move.)

William: Give up, Duncan.

Duncan: Never!

William: *(Sitting up on one elbow)* You have one checker left. I have all kings. Admit it, you're defeated.

Duncan: More time—I need more time.

William: Well, that's the one thing I do have plenty of . . .

(Terry walks in slowly. He's wearing a very worn bandanna around his neck. He sits down in William's chair and stares numbly at the floor. Duncan and William exchange glances.)

William: *(Sitting up and hanging his legs over the edge of the bed)* Well?

(Silence from Terry.)

Duncan: *(Back to the game)* See, I told you, you cannot work your way out of here.

Terry: *(Slowly looking up at Duncan and then William)* Rags, it's all just rags. *(Stands up, rips bandanna from his neck, and holds it up, clenched in his fist.)* He said all I've done is like filthy rags. My work amounts to nothing. I'll be here until I die! I owe more than when I came.

Duncan: Spare me the theatrics. We told you before not to expect so much. In debtors prison you can't pay for your own debts.

Terry: *(In anger and frustration, sweeps the checkerboard onto the floor, looks into Duncan's face.)* OK, if you have all the answers, then tell me—who can?

Duncan: *(Standing up face to face with Terry, hostile)* If I knew the answer to that question, do you think I would be standing here wasting my days in your company? *(Gesturing to William)* Or his?

William: *(Gently, to break the tension)* Someone able, who cares enough about you to pay your debt, that's who.

Duncan: *(Glaring at William)* And none of us knows anyone like that! *(Turns away and begins to pick up the checkers.)*

William: *(To Terry)* When Duncan's business began to fail, he asked his father-in-law for money. His father-in-law is the Duke of Hazards. He lives in the southern part of England and is a very wealthy man. The duke never cared for his daughter's marriage to a commoner, so instead of helping him, he allowed Duncan to be put in prison.

Duncan: Poor timing, really. I was about to enter into a partnership with an old Scottish farmer named Ronald. We were intending to open a new shop and name it after him: Ronald McDonald's. We were going to use my fresh bread and his meat to make a special sandwich named the McDuncan or Big Dunc or something like that. But, when my father-in-law would not help me out . . . (*His voice trails off.*)

Terry: (*Looking at Duncan*) I'm sorry Duncan. You shouldn't be in here.

William: None of us should. I would still be in my shop if my landlord had not decided he wanted to put a tavern there. He began to raise the rent until I could no longer pay. By the time I left, he had seized all my instruments. I had nothing with which to pay the back rent, the taxes, or the suppliers for my trade.

Terry: (*Sitting back down*) What're we going to do? We all owe so much. I owe so much. Two years' back rent on the land and a year of food from my brother. It would take a king's ransom to cover my debts. And I don't know anyone with that kind of money.

Duncan: Well, I do, and it doesn't make my situation any better.

Terry: My wife has written to all our relatives asking them for their help, but they all are in the same situation we are. Except, of course, they've not landed in here.

William: (*Jumping down from the bed*) Wait a minute, chaps, there was a fellow here once who told me a remarkable story. He had heard of a nobleman in the north of England who was known to despise debtors prisons. The story goes that the nobleman, whom I think was supposed to be a prince, liked to pay off prisoners' debts and thereby secure their release.

Terry: (*Looking up*) I think I've heard that story before. (*Thinking*) The nobleman was . . . the Duke of Northumberland.

Duncan: So what's the rest of the story?

William: (*Beginning to realize the importance of his story*) Apparently a prisoner some years ago wrote a letter to this duke.

Duncan: (*Intently*) And then?

William: They say that after a month or so this prisoner packed up and left.

Terry: (*With new hope*) He left alive!

William: Pardon me?

Terry: You said, "No one leaves alive." This man left alive.

Duncan: William! Why have you not remembered this?

William: I never really believed it could be true—thought it an old prisoner's wishful tale. Until now. (*Shrugging his shoulders*) Besides, when I first heard the story, you were ahead of me by 186 games in Checkers. I wanted a chance to catch up.

Terry: This is our only hope.

Duncan: (*With more life and energy than we've seen from Duncan so far*) We must contact this gentleman immediately.

William: I'll get the phone.

Duncan and Terry: The what?

(*Fade to black. Blues music up. Fade music out as lights come back up for scene 3.*)

SCENE 3

(*Scene opens with Duncan and William playing Checkers once again. There is a smattering of kings on the board, but the game is even. Duncan and William are somewhat distracted, however, and occasionally glance toward Terry. Terry is lying on the bench but gets up and crosses to the door, looking out the window. He paces nervously and looks uneasy.*)

Narrator: (*Offstage*) Duncan, Terry, and William did get a letter out of the prison to the Duke of Northumberland. They explained how their debts were impossible to pay on their own, and they asked for mercy. After that, all they could do was wait.

Duncan: (*After William moves a checker*) Now William, my friend, are you sure that's the move you want to make?

William: (*Innocently*) Why, whatever do you mean?

Duncan: It just seems like a rash move, and I'm quite willing to let you make that move again, if you feel for some reason that's not your best choice.

William: That's so considerate of you, Duncan. But I think I'll let my marker stay as it is.

Duncan: (*He moves a checker, growls.*) This game requires no skill whatsoever; it's just a matter of luck!

William: (*Jumps four checkers.*) Ahh...got lucky again. King me...

Terry: (*Impatiently*) Why has the Duke of Northumberland taken so long to reply? You would think he would at least acknowledge our letter.

Duncan: You're sure it was the Duke of Northumberland in the story?

Terry: (*Somewhat irritated*) Yes, yes. We've been through this before. (*Pause*) At least I think it was Northumberland.

Duncan: And William, you're certain that he paid the way for this other prisoner to be released?

William: (*Impatiently*) Yes, Duncan. Yes.

Terry: (*Sitting up*) Someone's coming.

(*They look at the edge of the stage expectantly, and the guard enters with a rolled-up sheet of paper.*)

Prison Guard: Terry Coppersmith?

Terry: (*Nervously*) Yes?

Prison Guard: I have a message from...(*looking at the edge of the scroll*) the Duke of Northumberland. (*He hands the scroll to Terry.*)

(Terry crosses to the front of the table holding the rolled-up message. Duncan and William stand up and come to either side of him. Terry should be right in front of William's chair. Terry holds the paper nervously.)

Duncan: *(Impatiently)* Don't wait all day, man, open it!

William: *(Gently)* Open it, Terry. Read to us what it says.

(Terry carefully unrolls the sheet of paper. He reads the first line silently and then sinks into the chair with a sense of hopelessness.)

Terry: *(Reading from the letter)* "Kind Sirs: On the 31st of May this past year, the Duke of Northumberland died..."*(He lowers the letter into his lap and looks at the floor.)*

Duncan: *(Disbelieving)* He's dead?

Terry: *(Weakly)* He's dead.

Duncan: *(Frustrated, sits down at the table as he speaks.)* Why did I let myself believe that someone else could ever cover my debts? No one cares, and we can no longer help ourselves. It's hopeless.

William: *(Taking the letter and holding it at arm's length to read it)* "Kind Sirs: On the 31st of May this past year, the Duke of Northumberland died. During the duke's life, he secured the release of many a ward from debtors prisons all across England. When the duke was a boy..."*(Continues reading to himself, muttering occasionally.)*

Terry: *(Quietly)* I'll never see my family again.

Duncan: *(To himself with disgust)* I do not know why I allow myself to get caught up in these irresponsible schemes.

Terry: I'll be here the rest of my life. In this room.

Duncan: *(As he studies the game, all business)* William, the game awaits.

William: *(Growing excited)* Listen to this! "But with the death of the Duke of Northumberland comes hope for many in the debtors prisons of England. For the entire estate and holdings of the duke are being used to secure the release of all prisoners at the Dunsmire Debtors Prison." *(Yells joyfully.)* His death secures our release. Duncan, Terry, we're free! *(Begins playing an imaginary violin and waltzes around the stage, humming, full of joy.)*

Duncan and Terry: *(Blankly)* The Dunsmire Debtors Prison?

William: *(Stopping for a second, pointing to the letter)* The release is secured for all prisoners at the Dunsmire Debtors Prison. *(Comes behind the table and slaps both of them on the back.)* My friends, we'll be free; we ARE free! Our debt is paid! *(He looks down at the game, pauses, then jumps a checker twice.)* I believe this game is mine, Duncan. *(He begins to waltz some more, playing the violin.)* I shall have a new store and make nothing but the finest instruments of exotic woods from around the world.

(As Terry stands up to deliver his lines, Duncan looks down at the game and quietly begins to reset.)

Terry: (*Grinning broadly*) I'll find a new farm. This is a new start, and I'll not waste it.

(*William's dancing has brought him to the door of the cell; he stops.*)

William: The door is open. (*Looking out*) Prisoners are running all over out there. Duncan, Terry, let us gather our possessions and go home! (*Both he and Terry quickly begin to gather up their things.*)

Terry: (*Laughing*) I can't wait to see the look on my wife's face.

William: (*Laughs*) The look on her face? I can't even remember what my wife looks like!

(*William and Terry both laugh again. As they turn to head for the door they notice Duncan, who is studying the checkerboard.*)

Duncan: (*To himself*) The key is not to sacrifice too many, too soon. Let the other player be aggressive.

William: (*Gently*) Duncan?

Terry: The door is open; we're free to go.

Duncan: (*Firmly, not harshly, not mournfully*) No one is interested in paying my debt. It's my concern. No one cares.

William: Ah, but that's no longer true, my friend. The death of one man has brought freedom for all.

Terry: Your debts are paid, Duncan. You're free. You have a fresh start. (*They move toward the door.*) Come with us. Come! (*Terry walks offstage.*)

William: (*Hesitates.*) Duncan, please come.

Duncan: I think not. You go.

William: Duncan . . . (*Pauses, then sadly*) Good-bye. (*Turns and leaves.*)

Duncan: (*Sighs as he pushes aside the checkerboard.*) I think I'll take up Chess.

(*Fade to black. Blues music comes up and then fades out.*)

THE END

ROSE'S COSTUME SHOP

BY DEAN NADASDY

"[Jesus said] 'If people want to follow me, they must give up the things they want. They must be willing even to give up their lives to follow me. Those who want to save their lives will give up true life. But those who give up their lives for me and for the Good News will have true life' "
(MARK 8:34-35).

THEME
Lent/Sacrifice.

SUMMARY
Four young people with roles in a high school production of Thornton Wilder's "Our Town" visit a costume shop, where they learn that they must "lose" themselves to become who God would have them be.

CHARACTERS
Rose–She is eager to teach, 80+ years old, and very much in control. Rose is mysterious and should be played by an older adult with acting skills.

Erwin–Also in his 80s, he is the surprise of the play and is best played by an older adult with acting skills.

Gina–She is apparently bold but is actually covering her insecurity with false confidence.

Emmet–A "blender," he fits in whatever crowd he is with; avoids conflict.

Molly–She is pretty, trendy, and self-aware.

Kenyon–He is full of smiles and humorous, but uses his wit as a defense against the world.

SETTING
A sales counter is at stage left. Two racks of costumes are at stage right. The racks include many more costumes than those necessary for the play. Signs are posted that read, "Welcome to Rose's Costumes," "Additional charges for late returns," "The play's the thing," and "Costumes make the actor."

PROPS
Turn-of-the-century women's high-top shoes, three-piece wool suit, suspenders, bow tie, pants and shirt, pipe, dress, clown costume, princess costume, tiara, hand-held mirror, camouflage outfit, scarecrow outfit, a glass of water, special makeup for Erwin, and four folding chairs. You'll also need appropriate stage lights and sound.

THE SCRIPT
"Rose's Costume Shop"

Rose: (*Stands behind counter at stage left and addresses audience; stays busy straightening counter as she talks.*) Welcome to my costume shop. I am Rose—the Rose of Rose's Costumes. My husband, Erwin, and I began the business in 1949. We are a small shop, but we do our best to provide the costumes for the schools and theater groups in our city. Unfortunately the costume business is not what it used to be. (*Steps around to front of counter to be closer to audience, looks around, uses stage whisper.*) Can you keep a secret? We may have to start renting out tuxedos soon. Penguin suits! Can you believe it? (*Straightens up, uses full voice.*) Now, as we consider this, the season of sacrifice that precedes the celebration of our Savior's resurrection, there's something I want you to know. There is a parallel in life and on the stage. On the stage the actor must sacrifice—must lose himself or herself in a role to discover the person behind the lines. In life we must lose ourselves in the life of our Lord, Jesus, to discover the person behind the Scriptures.

    (*Stops as voices of four young people are heard.*)

Rose: Oh, it sounds like they are already here. You see, Jack Marshall at the high school, he always—ah, well, I'm afraid we have no time for that now. Quickly, before they come into the shop. Just listen to Jesus' words from the Gospel of Mark. Are you listening? Well, are you? (*Waits for response from audience.*) Good. (*Speaks very slowly.*) Jesus said, "If people want to follow me, they must give up the things they want. They must be willing even to give up their lives to follow me." Did you get that? Yes? Good. (*Returns behind counter.*)

    (*Gina, Emmet, Molly, and Kenyon enter up center aisle of audience to the counter at stage left. Talking among themselves as they come.*)

Rose: May I help you?

Gina: Yes. We need some costumes. Mr. Marshall sent us over. We're putting on "Our Town".

Rose: Ah, "Our Town". A beautiful play—about living and dying, falling in love, marrying—about the simple beauties of life. Emily, sweet Emily, how...

Gina: That's my role! I'm Emily.

Rose: Sweet thing. There in the kitchen, back from the dying, taking it all in. It was much too much for her. And her love for young, ah, what's his name...

Gina: (*Impatiently*) Shoes!

Rose: Shoes! No, that wasn't his name. That couldn't have been his name.

Gina: No, I need shoes, period shoes for Emily. You know, the high-top kind.

Rose: (*Pulls shoes out from behind counter.*) Like these.

Gina: *(Amazed)* Exactly. Perfect in fact.

Rose: *(To Emmet)* And you, young man, what do you need?

Emmet: I need a period vested suit with a little padding. I'm Doc Gibbs.

Rose: *(Walks over to rack; pulls off suit.)* You are, indeed. *(Handing suit to Emmet)* Here you are, Doc. What else can we do for you?

Molly: I'm supposed to pick up a dress for Mrs. Gibbs.

Rose: This dress has been worn by many a Mother Gibbs, my dear. *(Picking dress from rack)* This will do, I'm sure.

Kenyon: And I'll need suspenders, pants, a bow tie, a shirt, and a pipe.

Rose: A pipe, no less. The Stage Manager, no doubt. *(Hands costume to Kenyon.)*

Kenyon: *(Surprised)* Yes. *(Takes costume.)* Thanks.
　　(Rose stares at Kenyon appraisingly.)

Rose: Yes, I believe you'll do quite well. And the costume will age you up just fine.

Kenyon: Thank you.

Gina: Mr. Marshall said you would just bill the school.

Rose: As always, child. *(Pauses.)* Don't you love it when Emily asks the Stage Manager, "Do any human beings ever realize life while they live it?—every, every minute?" And he says, "No...The Saints and poets, maybe—they do some." Goodness, children, we could use more poets and saints!

Gina: You certainly know the play, Miss...

Rose: Just call me Rose. Yes, I do know the play. Thornton Wilder wrote it, and it's done by just about every theater group at one time or another. That's why we have the costumes ready to go. The shoes are size 7, Emily.

Gina: Perfect.

Rose: So tell me, how go the rehearsals?

Kenyon: Mr. Marshall says we have a long way to go.

Rose: That sounds like Jack.

Gina: You know Mr. Marshall?

Rose: Let's just say I remember when he was here asking for those suspenders 20 years ago. *(Looks at the suspenders in Kenyon's hands.)*

Kenyon: He says we have to lose ourselves in our parts.

Rose: I know.

Kenyon: You do?

Rose: Of course, isn't that the challenge we always face when we want to become someone other than who we are?

Molly: Mr. Marshall says it's because we're too self-conscious—and that we'll never get it right until we lose ourselves and become the characters we're meant to be.

Rose: Sounds like he knows something about the theater. When Thornton wrote the play, he had in mind...

Molly: Thornton? Did you say Thornton? You knew Thornton Wilder?

Rose: I...

Molly: This is unbelievable.

Rose: I just know Mr. Wilder wanted real people in his play, real salt-of-the-earth people. You can't be real if you hang onto who you think people want you to be. You can't be two people at once. That's what Jack Marshall's saying. (*Under her breath as she begins to set up four folding chairs center stage, back to audience*) I taught him well.

Gina: (*Overhearing*) You taught Mr. Marshall?

Rose: Just as I'll teach you. Here, give me these. (*Takes costume pieces and lays them on counter.*) Now have a seat.

Gina: We really should be going. Mr. Marshall...

Rose: He knows you're here, child. Don't worry. Please.

(*Points to chairs. Gina, Emmet, Molly, and Kenyon hesitantly sit on chairs.*)

Rose: Good. Thank you. (*Stands directly in front of them, center stage.*) Now, I would like you to think of yourself. That's not hard. Here (*goes to get a large hand-held mirror from counter, hands it to Gina*), each of you take a good, hard look at yourself.

Gina: (*Looking in mirror*) As pretty as ever. (*Passes mirror to Kenyon.*)

Kenyon: (*Looking in mirror*) Funny guy, but your face is crooked! (*Passes mirror to Molly.*)

Molly: (*Looking in mirror*) OK, nothing I haven't seen before. (*Passes mirror to Emmet.*)

Emmet: OK. So now what? (*Hands mirror to Rose.*)

Rose: Think of what Mr. Marshall said. He said you will never get it right until you lose yourself and become the character you're meant to be. Right?

Kenyon: Yeah, so?

Rose: Think. What must you lose to become the character you're meant to be? What is there inside of you that you must face and put away for the sake of your character? Think. (*Paces for a silent count of about 20 seconds.*) Now, stand up, each of you, and walk over to the costume racks. (*Pointing to costumes*) Choose a costume that fits the part of you that must go. Go ahead. Take your time.

Kenyon: I don't get it. Are we talking about acting or are we talking about life?

Rose: There's a difference? Just go.

Emmet: I don't get it.

Molly: Let's just do what she says.

(*Gina, Emmet, Molly, and Kenyon go to the costume racks. As they rummage through costumes, Rose moves forward to speak to the audience. During her speech, Gina puts on a scarecrow costume [straw, tilted hat, broom, red bandanna, etc.], Emmet puts on a camouflage suit, Molly puts on a princess costume with a tiara, and Kenyon puts on a clown outfit. The costumes they put on should not be complete but enough to identify their characters.*)

Rose: Now, my friends, as it is in the theater, it is in life. We will never become who we're meant to be until we give up the parts of ourselves that hold us back. We've been doing this for years here—puttin' on and takin' off. And it simply will not do to allow ourselves to be held back. The Good Book says we must lose ourselves to find ourselves. I'm no preacher, but it sure makes sense to me. (*Looks around the shop.*) It's that way in the theater and in life as well. You children almost ready?

Gina: Just about.

Rose: (*Walks over to them.*) Ah, fine. Now, have a seat.

Emmet: Nice costume, Kenyon.

Kenyon: Happy Halloween.

Emmet: Hope nobody sees me in this.

Rose: Now tell us why you chose the costume you did. Who would like to start? (*No response*) Each of you has a reason. The costume tells us about some part of you that must be left behind. What is it?

Gina: This isn't easy. We don't even know you.

Emmet: I don't think we even know each other well enough.

Rose: But I know you. Maybe better than you know yourselves.

  (*All four students look at each other uncomfortably.*)

Kenyon: It's just—we didn't come to do this.

Rose: I know, dear. Humor an old woman. (*Silence*) What must you leave behind?

Kenyon: Well, I chose the clown costume. (*Looks out toward audience.*)

Emmet: That's obvious.

Rose: Yes, Kenyon, the clown costume. But why?

Emmet: Because he's a clown, that's why.

Rose: Is this true Kenyon?

Kenyon: (*Unwillingly*) Yes.

Rose: So say it. Say it—"I am a clown."

Kenyon: I am a clown. (*Looks to audience.*) Why do I feel that more people are watching me than just my friends?

Rose: Not to worry, young man. Stand and tell us. Why are you a clown? Come on.

Kenyon: (*Stands to face friends and audience.*) I spend most of my time trying to get laughs. I get attention that way. It makes me popular. I use my humor to stop from getting too serious or too close to others.

Rose: Does it work?

Kenyon: It's always worked for me. I'm the funny guy, the class clown, the one-liner king, but just once I'd like someone to take me seriously. To see that I'm more than just a funny guy. Just once... (*Wistfully trails off.*)

Rose: Yes, Kenyon, that was well said.

Molly: (*Quietly*) I take you seriously, Kenyon.

Kenyon: You do?

Molly: Sure. And people only see one side of me, too.

Rose: Is that why you chose that costume?

Molly: Yes, I wear the princess costume.

Rose: Tell us, child, why a princess?

Molly: Always the spotlight for me, always the awards and the recognition. Sometimes, though, it gets to be too much.

Rose: How could it be too much?

Molly: I feel I must always be picture-perfect. What a beauty! I want to be more than Princess Pretty.

Rose: (*Nodding her head*) And so you shall, and so you shall. And you, young man?

Emmet: I'm in camouflage because I'm always whatever everyone else wants me to be. I dress like the crowd, talk like the crowd, and blend in with the crowd. I am the crowd—a chameleon. I am one lost in many. (*Falters.*) Uh—it's your turn, Gina.

Rose: Gina?

Gina: I'm wearing the scarecrow costume because everyone thinks I'm so brave and courageous, but I'm not. I try everything, but on the inside I'm afraid. Everyone thinks I'm strong, but it's like I am really only straw. I fool the world the way a scarecrow fools the birds.

Rose: Well done, children. Now I ask you to take off your costumes, but before you do...(*She is interrupted by a noise offstage.*)

Erwin: (*Erwin enters down center aisle. He is costumed as if horribly beaten, with bruised features and shabby clothing, stumbling his way in. He stumbles to center stage and falls at feet of players.*) Help me, please.

Rose: My goodness, old man, what has happened?

Erwin: (*From floor*) They have beaten and robbed me, taken all my cash and my car. They left me for dead.

   (*The tempo of the play should pick up here.*)

Rose: Children, what do we do?

Emmet: I'll get some water. (*Goes offstage to get water.*)

Kenyon: Here, let's get him up on a chair.

Molly: Was your back hurt, Mister?

Erwin: No, my back is all right.

Kenyon: Come on, Molly... 1, 2, 3.

 (They lift Erwin at both arms; Erwin sits on chair.)

Emmet: Here, Mister, take a drink.

Erwin: *(Drinks from glass.)* Thank you. Thank you so much.

Gina: Have you called the police?

Erwin: They're on the way.

Gina: *(Taking red bandanna from scarecrow outfit)* Let me wipe your face.
 (Dabs Erwin's face without removing his makeup.)

Erwin: Again, I thank you.

Kenyon: What else can we do for you, sir?

Erwin: Well, you—*(looking at Rose)*—you, uh...

 (Rose shakes head in approval; Erwin stands and smiles.)

Erwin: You can tell me why you have those silly looking costumes on!

Gina: What in the world?

Erwin: *(To Rose)* How did I do, sweetheart?

Rose: *(To Erwin)* One of your finest performances, my dear.

Kenyon: Who is this?

Rose: This is my husband, Erwin.

Gina: And the robbery and his injuries?

Rose: All an act, I'm afraid.

Erwin: Well crafted—and finely costumed, too. One of these years, I ought to get some sort of an award for a man my age acting with such Thespian prowess. Why, I...

Emmet: But why? Why the act?

Rose: Listen, my young friends, and listen well. There you were, costumed up in that part of you that must die if you are ever to become who you're meant to be. And suddenly there came someone in need, someone who called for love and action that was real and from the heart. And what did you do?

Molly: We acted. We did what needed to be done.

Rose: And you forgot your costumes. You forgot yourselves, didn't you?

Kenyon: We did.

Gina: And that's what has to happen in the play, right?

Kenyon: *(With understanding)* That's what has to happen in our lives.

Rose: Exactly. What has old Erwin here taught you?

Gina: We must lose ourselves and act from the heart.

Emmet: And when you act from the heart, you act in love. Then you begin to become who you are meant to be.

Gina: You knew, didn't you, Rose? You knew we were coming!

Rose: It is our secret, those of us who do this every year. Jack Marshall sends us students who have yet to learn that when we love, we lose ourselves and find a life that's real. It is the secret of the theater and the secret of life. Keep it between us—Will you, children?—for others will come.

Gina: We will.

Emmet: We promise.

Rose: Now you may take off those costumes, leave them behind, and go and be Emily, and Doc Gibbs, and Mother Gibbs, and the Stage Manager. Oh yes, and before you leave, there's something I want you to know. *(Looking to audience, then to the four)* There is a parallel in life and on the stage. On the stage the actor must sacrifice—must lose himself or herself in a role to discover the person behind the lines. In life, we must lose ourselves in the life of our Lord, Jesus, to discover the person behind the Scriptures.

Gina: I never thought of it like that before, Rose.

Rose: Now take off those costumes, friends, and be on your way.

>   *(The four go to racks and remove costumes.)*

Erwin: How much longer am I going to be doing this, my love?

Rose: Are you getting tired?

Erwin: We've had a long run with this show, Rosie. How much longer?

Rose: As long as God's children must learn the power of Jesus' sacrifice and grow in the power of their own sacrifice, we'll have our little stage. *(Moves to counter, hands the "Our Town" costumes to the four.)* Now be on your way.

Gina: *(Taking shoes)* Thank you, Rose. *(Embraces Rose.)*

Rose: Back to the stage with all of you.

Kenyon: Thanks.

Molly: We'll see you again.

Rose: I hope so.

Emmet: Later.

Rose: Yes, later. Now off with you.

>   *(Gina, Kenyon, Molly, and Emmet exit center aisle through audience. When characters are all gone, Rose turns to audience.)*

Rose: What? You still here? *(Laughs.)* We'll see you again, too. But for now, be on your way. You've got a lot of living, and giving, yet to do.

>   *(Lights fade.)*

THE END

THE MOTHERS HALL OF FAME

BY JULIANNE BRUCE

"No one else can know your sadness, and strangers cannot share your joy" **(PROVERBS 14:10).**

THEME

Mothers.

SUMMARY

Using examples of biblical women, these monologues follow from birth to death some of the major events and decisions that a mother might face in the course of raising her children.

CHARACTERS

Narrator–A person to introduce the play.

Bathsheba–Bathsheba is the town gossip. She's the one you see at the back fence talking to all the neighbors. She's a very animated character. She thinks that each detail of the story she's spreading is the most important part, so every nuance is extremely exaggerated. This time, she's the one the gossip is about, and she's just dying to be the one to spread the news—confidentially, of course.

Rebekah–Rebekah is an up-and-coming businesswoman, a typical '80s yuppie. She speaks sharply, which reveals her cold cunning and her disregard for feelings or emotions. Everything in her life revolves around her desire to get ahead. Now that she has a son, Jacob, who is much like herself, those plans include him.

Eve–Eve is a farmer's wife, in the tradition of Minnie Pearl. She speaks in a slow, thoughtful drawl, using expansive language and gestures. She is simple and has yet to learn the ways of the world. Like most mothers, Eve is trying her best, but things aren't working out the way she had hoped they would.

Sarah–Sarah is a wise woman who has trouble applying her wisdom to her own life. She knows she should trust God and her husband, yet her own insecurities make it difficult for her. She wants to understand everything that's going on, so she comes across as both nagging and whiny in trying to get information. She thinks knowing everything now will help her trust God more.

Naomi–Naomi's life has taken some nasty turns. As a result, she's become one of those nagging, whining mothers who thinks everyone is against her. She feels entirely put upon, as though life is just one big trial after another. Her tone is completely sarcastic. She just can't see past her own bitterness until Ruth, who she's been against from the start, finds a way to soften her heart. Even then, she has a hard time admitting that life could turn out all right.

Mary–Mary is a woman who has survived much pain. She is strong, but watching her son die has drained her strength. She remembers the best parts about being a mother and openly mourns her loss. In the end she is left with memories and questions, but also with hope.

SETTING/PROPS

There are six different locations for this play, but none of them needs to be more than a suggestion using props. What is most important is that the tone for each character is visually set. Bathsheba can talk over a white picket fence. Rebekah needs nothing more than an office chair and a briefcase. Eve should have a spade and a sack labeled "fertilizer" to suggest her working in her garden. Sarah can sit at her kitchen table, drinking a cup of coffee. Naomi should be in a rocking chair, and Mary needs to have a representation of a cross in the background.

Place the six locations in different areas on the stage, staggering their positions. Each character should be lit only while she is speaking. If the lighting can't be adjusted that much, have each character sit with her back turned when she is not speaking.

THE SCRIPT
"The Mothers Hall of Fame"

Narrator: In the pages of the Bible, we find recorded the stories of mothers who've been through it all—they've experienced joy and sadness, disappointment and triumph, fear and confidence. Wouldn't it be great if we could gather some of these mothers in one place to listen in on their thoughts and experience the highs and lows of motherhood with them? Although in real life this is impossible, anything can happen on a stage. So without further ado, journey with me into the world of possibility as I introduce some very special guests for today.

(*Each character stands as she is introduced.*)

Narrator: Bathsheba: King David's wife and the mother of King Solomon. Rebekah: mother of those famous twins Esau and Jacob. Eve: the first mother. Sarah: whose long awaited son was almost sacrificed. Naomi: a mother who lost her natural children. Mary: arguably the most famous mother in history—the mother of Jesus. Now, sit back and let yourself enter into their world as they tell us their stories.

(*Lights come up on Bathsheba.*)

Bathsheba: (*As though answering a completely obvious question about her son*) King Solomon? My son? Of course I'm proud of him! What mother wouldn't be? He comes from such an impressive bloodline, you know. (*In a confidential tone*) Not that he has the purest of all backgrounds. Oh no! It's quite the sordid story! I tell you I wouldn't have believed it if it hadn't happened to me! (*With mock surprise over the whole situation*)

There I am, minding my own business, when suddenly one of King David's men is at my door! *(Stands and turns back partly to the audience and then turns out. She relives the story as she tells us.)* Me? The king wants to see me? Now? Whatever for? *(Back to gossipy tone)* Well, it turns out of all things that he saw me bathing! I must say I was mortified. *(Coming to juicy part, although trying to act like she's accidentally letting the details discreetly slip out)* But you know, we started talking, and he's really such a charmer, and as it turns out... well, one thing led to another... and another to another, and a few weeks later I find out I'm, well *(pause)*, pregnant! And, again, I am just mortified. Me, pregnant, while my husband, Uriah, is away fighting in the war for King David! *(With disgust, as though she doesn't see herself as a gossip)* Just think of the talk around Jerusalem. You know how some people are in this town! *(Back to the story, with a flippant attitude about the whole problem)* So I send a note to King David—discreetly, of course—and tell him of my, um, you know, "delicate situation." The penalty for this kind of indiscretion is death, but with him being the king and all, I figure he can find a way around our little problem. But instead of help from David, I just get a message... *(sitting down as if in shock)* Uriah is dead. Do you know how it happened? *(Waits for response, then nods her head slowly.)* Cut down while fighting on the front lines. That does sound like him. *(Turns away.)* What will I do now? *(Slowly works her way back to the gossipy tone)* Luckily, while I'm trying to figure this all out, David sends for me, and we get married. I'm sure that must have started a few tongues wagging—the way people gossip around here, it's just sinful! So then, several months later, I give birth to this darling little boy. I must say, he's just the cutest little thing in the world. I just can't help but adore him—*(dryly)* no matter how he got here.

Of course David simply adores his new son, too—as if he could feel any other way! But then one day he tells me some man named Nathan came to see him—he's supposed to be a prophet or something. *(Turns and relives the event, angrily.)* What do you mean our baby will die! I don't care what God told this prophet. Don't talk to me about sin—this is on your head. I was just taking a bath! Why should I suffer? *(Now showing a bit more of her true feelings, a little remorse and some sadness)* Apparently God didn't see it that way, though, and my darling baby got sick and died. *(Back to the gossipy tone)* But, you know, the Lord isn't completely unfair, and pretty soon he gave us another baby—a boy again. David simply treasured our little Solomon, and I just knew that he was going to grow up to be something special—as if any son of mine wouldn't. And Solomon has been so precious. Despite the pain and heartache, God has worked out our lives for his best.

(Lights fade out, and come back up on Rebekah.)

Rebekah: (*As though cradling her baby in her arms*) Finally, after all this time, I have a son to carry on the family line. I've been waiting for you a long time, Jacob. I wanted you to arrive right after your father and I got married, but my plans were somewhat postponed. Your father and I prayed and prayed, and it must have done some good because finally, here you are. You are a gift from God. (*Looks offstage as if hearing something.*) You and your brother, that is. (*Calls offstage.*) Miriam, can't you hear Esau crying? Please take care of him, will you? I'm busy.

Yes, Jacob, that's your brother crying. The two of you don't like each other much, do you? From the moment you were conceived, you fought each other inside of me. That didn't make for an easy pregnancy, but I know how hard it must have been for you. Don't worry, though. You won't have to share anything with Esau ever again. (*Smugly*) Yes, I think you already have a sense of your place in this world. Esau was born first, but you followed right behind. You had hold of his heel, as though you didn't want him to get the better of you. (*Calls offstage with an edge to her voice as if answering someone.*) Well, if he's hungry, feed him. I said I'm busy! (*With a proud smile*) That's the last time you'll ever have to be second to Esau. You had to follow, but just once. It's part of the prophecy. The Lord told me, "The older will serve the younger." And Esau will serve you, if I have anything to say in the matter. I know where your destiny lies. (*Comes to the front of the stage as if looking out a window.*)

I'll teach you everything I know, and then I'll find men who can continue to guide you, like my brother, Laban. Already your father favors Esau. He'll probably teach him to hunt and work the fields, but that's not for you. You need to be educated. I want you to be prepared.

You are special, Jacob. Don't forget that. God has something for you, and I want to be a part of it. I'll teach you never to miss an opportunity to get ahead. Always stay one step in front of everyone else, no matter what the cost. You're going to be strong. You deserve the best, and you'll have it. It won't always be easy, but in the end you'll appreciate all I've done for you. I just want the best for you.

(*Lights fade out and come back up on Eve.*)

Eve: Land sakes! I surely don't know what to do with them two boys o' mine. Every year it seems to get worse! (*Yells offstage.*) Cain, git offa your brother this instant! No, Abel, Abel, I...(*winces*) well you boys had bett'r clean that up! (*Normal voice*) Cain makes Abel mad, and then Abel gets him back, and vicey versy. Why, jus' the other day Abel went and swiped Cain's favorite hat. 'Course he didn't mean no harm, but Cain couldn't resist returnin' the favor. That night Cain went out, and he found himself a big ol' snake, and he put it in Abel's bed. It weren't no bitin' kind of snake, mind you, but it was a snake all the same. 'Course I was the one who stumbled onto that ugly critter, and I jus' hate them snakes. (*Pauses and shudders.*) Sometimes them boys go too far!

When they was little, they played together jus' fine. Oh sure, they got into scrapes now and again, but I figured that's the way children are gonna act. I mean, how am I supposed to know? With my two being the first boys ever, I can't rightly find me a book on it yet. But it's hard to tell sometimes when you oughta break it up and when you gotta let them work it out 'emselves. (*Calling offstage*) Hey, put that down. Abel, don't whack yer brother with that. You're gonna kill someone. I mean it. Put it down! (*Normal voice*) I mean, you can hear 'em a-yellin' and a-fightin' in the next room like a coupla wolf pups over an ol' bone, and when you go in to see what the squallin's about, they're all angel-eyed and innocent. (*Falsetto little boy's voice*) "Ain't nothin' going' on, Ma . . . really!" And even though their clothes are all mussed and one of 'em's a-bleedin', what're you supposed to do? At least they're on the same side, even if it is jus' 'til you turn yer back.

Seems to me they're always competin'. I reckon it's on account of them being brothers and all, but it's always over who can milk the fastest or which one can climb up that big ol' apple tree or who can fetch the water the quickest. (*Laughing*) Sure gets a heap of work done around here, though! (*Pause*) But all the hollerin' and bickerin' does rattle my nerves now and again. I don't think either of them means any harm. I reckon a mother just worries what might come of it. Being brothers I figure they're always gonna be tryin' to one-up each other. They jus' approach life so differently. Everything from what they like to do aft'r the chores are done to how they understand God, our creator. I think it's their differences that they're always tryin' to work out with their fists. But it does seem like they fight too much. (*Sighs.*) I've tried everythin' I could think of to make them boys be good. I finally told Adam that we jus' had to do somethin' to get them boys' minds onto things besides themselves. We pondered it for a long spell, rackin' our brains for some sorta fix-it. We finally figured puttin' Cain to work in the fields and havin' Abel tend the stock might jus' do it. I think that's a right good idea! I don't think they'll be able to find a way to compete doin' such different jobs. Maybe things will settle down a bit now. (*Yells offstage.*) Cain, where's Abel going? (*Pauses.*) Yes, I expect you to know—you're the oldest, and you oughta keep an eye out fer yer brother!

Well, jus' this morning I heard 'em talking to Adam about makin' a sacrifice to the Lord from their labors. Now that's the kind o' talk a mother likes to be hearin' from her boys. Maybe we've turned the corner on this siblin' rivalry stuff. Yes, I think this might turn out to be a nice, quiet year after all . . .

(Lights fade out and come back up on Sarah.)

Sarah: *(Pacing the floor, wringing her hands, and speaking in a scolding tone)* Abraham, I wish you'd talk to me about this. I'm your wife, after all, and I think you should tell me what's going on. Especially when it's about Isaac. All you've said is "trust the Lord." Well, that hardly gives me anything to go on. Abe? Abe, are you listening to me?

(Trying to put the pieces together) What happened last night when you talked to the Lord? *(Pauses.)* When you came in, you were pacing around and biting your nails, and I know you didn't sleep well. I sure didn't, with you thrashing around like that. The Lord must have said something that bothered you. Why won't you tell me what it is? Is it bad? *(Pauses.)* It's bad, isn't it? I knew it. I wish you wouldn't be so protective. Abraham, exactly what did the Lord say to you last night? *(Trying to pry it out of him)* It's obvious you're taking Isaac on a trip. I'm not blind, you know. So what kind of trip is it? A hunting trip? A pilgrimage? A father and son vacation? *(Harder)* Abraham, will you please stop packing and answer me?

(Pauses.) Trust the Lord? Trust the Lord? What does that mean? The last two times you've said that, we've moved! *(Muttering to herself)* Trust the Lord—that doesn't help. *(Back to Abraham)* I need more, dear. How about some details? *(To herself in exasperation)* I pray for years and years and years, and the Lord finally gives me a son. Now that I have him, I'm left out of the most important parts of his life. *(Sarcastically)* Sure, Abraham, take him on a trip. No, you don't need to tell me a thing. I'm not worried. I'm only his mother!

(As though looking out a window) Abraham, why are the servants bringing your religious clothes? Are you going to have some sort of ceremony? A sacrifice? Surely I didn't miss a holy day. Is that what God talked to you about? Do we need to teach Isaac something about the rituals? We haven't been lazy about his education, Abraham. I know we haven't. What does God think the problem is? We love Isaac too much to make such a huge mistake. Why, you're devoted to Isaac the way you're devoted to the Lord! You practically worship that boy! I know he's learning just what he should be.

(Pauses.) What? Yes, Abraham, you've said that several times. Trust the Lord. Are you talking to me or to yourself? I do trust him. You know I do. I suppose he wouldn't have waited all this time to give us a son only to let something happen to him. It's just that I can't help worrying. He's still my baby. *(Finally giving in)* OK. If you're going to make me sit at home and fret while you gallivant all over the countryside with our son, fine. All I ask is that you promise to bring him back in one piece.

(Lights fade out and come back up on Naomi.)

Naomi: (*Talking to her husband who has died*) Well, my husband, this may be hard to believe, but I think things might finally be getting better around here. And you know our life has been hard, right from the start! Why my mother named me Naomi, I'll never know. It means "pleasant," for Pete's sake! Was that supposed to be some sort of cosmic joke or something? Every day seemed to bring more hardship. There's been nothing pleasant about our life. I kept thinking things should turn around—but you know, I've been waiting a long time. Especially these past few years. Not only was it bad enough that there was that famine in Israel, but then you moved us all to Moab. (*Sarcastically*) Great place! What if Israel went to war with them again and then all my relatives would be attacking us in our new home?

(*Huge sigh*) Oh well, at least I had you and the kids with me. Except, of course, that you dropped dead and left me to fend for myself in that pagan wasteland. (*Shaking her head*) You wouldn't believe the neighbors we had! You remember what happened next? Mahlon, our good Hebrew son, goes and falls for some Moabite named Ruth. (*Sarcastically*) Great choice! (*Delivers her lines as if she is talking to her son.*) "What's the matter with you," I say to him. "You can't find some nice Hebrew girl to marry? Maybe you should cut your hair and get rid of those earrings." "But, Mom," he says. "Don't 'but, Mom' me," I tell him. "I won't have it! You must marry within our faith!" He just shrugged his shoulders and said it wasn't forbidden by law so who am I to forbid it? (*Big sigh*) What do you think of that?

(*Thinking out loud*) She must have put some kind of a spell on him. She wasn't any kind of good Hebrew girl. No, she must have had magic ways from that pagan religion of hers. Sure, now we can continue the family line, but it will never work out. So who listens to poor old ma? Nobody. In fact, not only does Mahlon marry this Ruth girl, but my dear little Kilion marries one of them, too! Orpah's her name. Just great! Now I've got two Moabite daughters. You know neither of them is good enough for my sons. Oh, husband, why couldn't we have just stayed in Israel?

Of course, I figured I was being punished for something. And it must've been something really awful because then both of our sons died, leaving me with these two girls. I didn't want them in the first place, so why should I want them now? It's not like they even gave me one grandchild between them. So what's the point? Are you keeping up with all this, husband? But just in time, I hear that the famine is over and I decide to go back home to live out my last terrible days. And the girls decide to follow me! Those girls kept right on my heels, just like puppies. I told them, "Go home. Find another husband, already." But they just cried and said they wanted to come with me. Just great!

I told them, "No, really, I mean it. Go home!" They weren't taking me seriously so I said, "What, you think I'm going to have more sons for you to marry? Take a hike!" They still refused to turn around, so I told them, "The Lord is against me!" But what kind of scare does that put into gentile girls? Maybe Orpah had heard about Moses and the plagues or something because she finally changed her mind and left. So then it was just Ruth.

She tells me, (*mimicking Ruth*) "Don't make me go back. I'll go with you no matter what." I told her, "Hey, kid, the well's dry." And she says, (*mimicking Ruth*) "The only way I'll ever leave you is to die."

(*Giving in*) I didn't really want to be responsible for this one, but suddenly she seemed like maybe she was actually sincere. I wondered if she had changed or if maybe I'd misjudged her. After all, it's a lot for a young, pretty thing like that to give up all her chances for a decent life and go with her crabby old mother-in-law.

So I thought maybe I'd give it a try. And, much to my surprise, Ruth turned out to be a very sweet girl. Maybe my son wasn't such a stupid kid after all. I mean, the girl carried my suitcases and let me have the first drink of water and generally redeemed herself. I figure she must have had some Jewish blood in her somewhere.

(*Starting to relax a little*) Once we reached Bethlehem, she really outdid herself. She went into the fields and gathered grain for us. Talk about your dangerous work! But she never complained. (*Aside*) I think she's starting to take after me. After awhile I started wondering what was it I had against this one, anyway? And I bragged to all my friends what a wonderful daughter-in-law she was. Ruth was such a good girl that I just couldn't help myself. She spent all her time trying to make my life, dare I say it, pleasant. (*Laughs at her own joke.*) So I thought I ought to do something for her. She seemed generally content, so I wasn't sure what to get her. Then it came to me. A husband! The girl needs a husband! So I kind of fixed her up with that long-lost cousin of yours, Boaz.

And if I do say so myself, things worked out rather nicely. Ruth has settled in with Boaz, and they've let me stay with them. I guess if you follow God long enough you start to see how he brings all the loose ends together. And you know what, husband? Our son was a better judge of people than I thought he was. Hard to believe, I know, but Ruth turned out to be just like the daughter I never had. She kind of reminds me of myself at that age. Now if only my bedroom was a little bigger, and you know, my window is right next to that barn. You'd think they'd care for an old woman in her last days better than that. Ah, well, such is my lot in life.

(*Lights fade out and come back up on Mary.*)

Mary: (*Talking slowly, as if in a state of confusion*) He's dead. I don't understand. God wouldn't let that happen. He wouldn't. Jesus was his Son. How could God let them kill his Son? My son! (*Crying out as perhaps she did at the cross*) No, Lord! Do something! Save him! Oh please, God, he's my son, too! (*Almost crying*) Why did they kill him? Why? Couldn't they see he was telling the truth? How many more people did he have to heal? Didn't he raise enough people from the dead? Why couldn't they see it?

(*Looking off as though seeing into the past*) Jesus—he was so special to me. Not because he was the Messiah, but because he was mine. A part of me. I told him stories and kissed his skinned knees. He came to me when he discovered something new and wanted to share it. I held him and took care of him. I loved him. And it ends here? Is this all there is?

(*Sadly*) How am I supposed to go on? How does a mother watch her child die and then go on? (*A little angry*) Am I supposed to act like nothing's happened? Mourn for a while and then pick up where I left off? I can't. (*Pauses, then quietly*) I'll never get over this.

(*After a long pause, then almost with a smile*) But no matter how much this hurts, I suppose I should be glad for the time we had. My precious son. I'll never see him again. But I'll never stop loving him. Never. And I'll never stop missing him. (*Sighs.*) I wanted him for me. God, his Father, wanted him for the whole world.

(*Looks up quickly as if startled. A look of recognition is registered on her face, followed by growing joy.*) Jesus, my son? Oh, your hands are hurt so badly. (*Starts as if to go to him but is caught short by the realization of who he is. She bows, then whispers.*) You are no longer dead. Messiah, you are your Father's Son.

(*Lights fade out.*)

THE END

LATE SHOW WITH DWIGHT LETTERBOY

BY TOM TOZER

....

"Honor your father and mother"

(EXODUS 20:12).

THEME
Fathers.

SUMMARY
This is a parody on the David Letterman show format, complete with drummer Saul (a one-man band), guests, and some of the off-the-wall features that Letterman does.

CHARACTERS
(Many roles can be played by the same people, if necessary.)

Dwight Letterboy–Dwight is the host. He is lively, energetic, and has a tongue-in-cheek delivery. (**Director's Note:** Dwight carries the show. He must be your strongest actor who can play his part with energy and pizazz.)

Saul–Saul is Dwight's drummer and one-man band. He should also have sparkle in his delivery.

Adman–The Adman is played by a male or female who can deliver the lines deadpan, enthusiastically, seriously, or however the pitch requires.

Dad 1–This guy is the dad who tells corny jokes a mile a minute and is his own best audience.

Dad 2–He is a real warm, expressive fellow.

Son 1–He is embarrassed by his father's overt affection.

Dad 3–Saul's dad; this fellow is fun-loving and doesn't take life too seriously. He is able to do a bird whistle.

Girl 1–A teenager.

Guy 1–A teenager.

Girl 2–A teenager.

Son 2–He is about 15 years old.

Dad 4–This is Son 2's father; probably 40 or so.

Dad 5–This is Dad 4's father; 65 or older.

(**Director's Note:** While not absolutely necessary, it would be a nice touch if Son 2, Dad 4, and Dad 5 were actually related.)

SETTING
The play takes place on the set of Dwight Letterboy's talk show. This can be performed easily in the chancel area or from the pulpit and lectern, with an occasional trip into the first few rows of the audience (congregation). There needs to be an elevated desk near the center with a chair for Dwight and another chair for the guest. This set could be on a platform. Saul can be at either stage right or left. Actors can enter from either side or upstage.

PROPS

Upbeat music; recorded applause; a placard with Top 10 List, each item covered so that it can be removed as Dwight names it off; an easel for the placard; a drum and drumstick for Saul; an awful-looking tie for the first commercial; a cardboard cutout of a TV screen for Son 1; a belt (preferably a long one) for the second commercial; Maalox bottle for the third commercial; a microphone for Dwight, especially when he goes into the audience (optional, depending upon each church's acoustics); and photocopied lyrics to "The F-A-T-H-E-R Song" on page 109. You'll need appropriate stage lights and sound.

THE SCRIPT
"Late Show With Dwight Letterboy"

(Girl 1, Guy 1, and Girl 2 are "plants" already seated in the audience. As people come in, give each woman and child in the audience a copy of "The F-A-T-H-E-R Song" handout.)

(Upbeat music starts as lights go up on Dwight's set.)

Adman: *(With enthusiasm)* And now, it's time for your favorite show, and your mother's, too...the Late Show With Dwight Letterboy! *(Applause.)*

Dwight: *(Moving front and center)* Thank you, thank you. Welcome to our special program on dads, otherwise known as "the Old Man," "the Big Guy," and the ever-reliable family savings and loan. Dad is the guy who is partially responsible for who we are—but we love him anyway.

(Saul does a one-stick rim-shot.)

Dwight: Fathers are strong believers in tradition. They like to hand things down from generation to generation—like chores.

(Saul does rim-shot.)

Dwight: Just kidding. Take my dad, for instance. He's been visiting me for a few days, and just last night I dropped him off at the airport. 'Course his plane doesn't leave 'til the day after tomorrow!

(Saul does another rim-shot.)

Dwight: Well, I hope you'll enjoy our show tonight as we take some time to poke fun at and honor our dads. We have lots of interesting guests and special features coming your way, so hang in there, and we'll be right back after this important message.

Adman: *(Enters; speaks in an unemotional tone.)* Need a quick Father's Day gift? *(Yawning)* Get your dad...another tie. *(Holding up bad tie)* Ties are uncomfortable. They're tight, they pinch, they're hot and sweaty. Your dad deserves no more, no less, so stock up. This Father's Day, don't surprise your dad at all. *(Yawning)* Get him another tie. *(Exits.)*

Dwight: We are pleased as all get out to have with us a special dad who won first place in the "Dads Who Tell Bad Jokes—Not Once but Over and Over" contest. Let's bring him on.

(Saul does a series of rim-shots. Dad 1 comes out, bows, and sits in the chair. Dwight sits behind the desk.)

Dad 1: Bet I can stick out my tongue and touch the back of my head.

Dwight: No way, Pops.

(Dad 1 sticks out his tongue, then touches the back of his head with his finger. He laughs.)

Dwight: Hey, that was bad, Dad!

Dad 1: You wanna hear a couple of dillies?

Dwight: Now we're gettin' somewhere. Shoot!

Dad 1: Dilly-dilly. *(Laughs harder.)*

Dwight: Wow. It's becoming clear why you won first place in our contest. *(Afraid to ask)* You don't by chance have another one, do you?

Dad 1: I know how to get your goat.

Dwight: Yeah? How?

Dad 1: I just watch where you tie it! *(Laughs even harder.)*

Dwight: *(Stands.)* Oh, Dad, stop, my sides are aching. *(To audience)* Actually, it's my head that's aching. *(Shaking hands with Dad 1)* Glad to meet you—happy Father's Day. My sympathies to your family. Let's hear it for him, folks!

(Dad 1 waves and exits as Saul does his anemic rim-shots.)

Dwight: Folks, it's time for some real humor—with our Top 10 Father's Day list. Saul, drumroll please!

(Saul does a drumroll of sorts. Dwight takes out a placard on an easel. He uncovers each answer as he announces it.)

Dwight: Here are the top 10 things that make dad...DAD.

Number 10: Wears dress socks with shorts.

Number 9: Knees crack every time he exhales.

Number 8: Starts every speech with "When I was your age..."

Number 7: Stands on scales but can't see numbers.

Number 6: Thinks Dagwood Bumstead is an overachiever.

Number 5: Refuses to let anyone else use the remote control.

Number 4: Puts the dad on the Brady Bunch right up there with St. Peter.

Number 3: Prays the longest at mealtime.

Number 2: Suffers under the misconception that moving elbows up and down fast is jogging.

And the Number 1 thing that makes dad DAD is...he brought you home from the hospital! Let's pause for this commercial message.

Adman: *(Enters; holds up belt.)* Kids, for Father's Day, do not—I repeat— do not get your dad a belt. One size does not fit all. As time goes by, less and less of it will be visible. Remember, a dad's waist is a terrible thing to mind. *(Exits.)*

Dwight: We're back. Our next guest is a dad from the national organization known as DWETC, or Dads Who Embarrass Their Children. And we also have his son who is joining us via satellite. Let's welcome them.

(Saul does a rim-shot. Dad 2 comes out, bows, and sits. Son 1 enters, stands behind Dwight, and looks at the audience through the cardboard cutout of a TV screen.)

Dwight: So, Dad, I understand you have a habit of making your kids feel pretty goofy.

Dad 2: I don't mean to. I'm just an affectionate guy.

(Son 1 frowns.)

Dwight: What about it, Son? *(Turns to screen.)*

Son 1: Hey, the guy won't shake hands—he bear-hugs me in public!

Dwight: Well, Dad, what do you have to say? Your son wants to shake hands.

Dad 2: *(Proudly)* I love my son—he's my boy!

Son 1: Well I love you, too. It's just that every time I come to visit, it's like championship wrestling! Can't we just greet each other like grown ups?

Dad 2: OK, OK, so I'll knock off the hugs! *(Shaking his head)* The older we get, the colder we get. What a world!

Son 1: Thanks, Pop.

Dad 2: Yeah, yeah, I hear ya. Now come by and visit, don't stay away so long—you haven't visited in months! And write your mother—tell her you're still eating your fiber!

Son 1: *(Shaking his head)* Oh, for Pete's sake. *(Disappears from screen and exits.)*

Dwight: *(Stands and extends his hand.)* Thanks for joining us, Dad.

(Dad 2 stands, goes over, and gives Dwight a bear hug. Dwight stiffly hugs him back. Dad 2 waves and exits. Dwight wipes his brow.)

Let's pause for this important Father's Day word while I adjust my back!

Adman: *(Comes out and holds up bottle.)* Maalox! *(Exits.)*

Dwight: We're back! Saul, what special thing do you remember about your dad?

Saul: That's easy. When I was a kid, we used to say a little prayer that went like this:

Thank you for the world so sweet.

Thank you for the food we eat.

Thank you for the birds that sing.

Thank you, God, for everything.

After the line about the birds that sing, Dad would do a chirping sound or hoot like an owl. On special occasions, he'd do Woody Woodpecker!

Dwight: (*Feigning horror*) That's wonderfully appalling!

Saul: It drove Mom up the wall. But Dad would say, "You know, kids, I'll bet God gets pretty tired of hearing the same old prayer over and over—he probably appreciates a little variety."

Dwight: Well, Saul, we have a little surprise for you. Your own father was the winner of our recent contest entitled "Dads Who Make Their Kids Laugh Out Loud During Quiet Moments at Church." And he's with us right now! Let's welcome Saul's dad!

(*Saul reacts with surprise. Dad 3 enters, waves to audience, shakes Dwight's hand, and meets Saul near center stage. Saul and his dad start to hug, then stop; start to shake hands, then stop; start again to hug, then stop; start again to shake hands, then stop. Finally, they both shrug and give each other a little wave. They all stand at center, with Dwight on the left, mike in hand, Dad 3 in center, and Saul at right.*)

Dwight: Well, Saul's Dad, it's nice to have you here. I understand you're going to lead our audience in one of your bird imitations.

Dad 3: Sure. This one is your simple, basic chirp. (*Does it.*) Everyone try it. (*He cues audience.*) OK, now let's all recite this wonderful little prayer together, and after "Thank you for the birds that sing," we'll all chirp!

Dwight: This will truly be a religious experience, ladies and gentlemen.

Saul: (*To audience*) Once you do it, you'll never be able to go back to the old way of returning thanks.

Dad 3: OK, everybody, let us pray!

(*Everyone recites prayer, following Dad 3's direction.*)

Thank you for the world so sweet.

Thank you for the food we eat.

Thank you for the birds that sing (*leads audience in chirping*).

Thank you, God, for everything.

Dad 3: That was great!

Dwight: We keep this up, folks, and this congregation just may win the "PEW-litzer Prize" for poetry! (*Shaking hands with Dad 3*) Well, Saul's Dad, this has been most enlightening, but fortunately that's all the time we have. Thanks for coming.

(*Saul and Dad 3 go through the same awkward pantomime as before. Dad exits, and Saul returns to his position.*)

Dwight: We'll be right back, but first this important public service message.

Adman: (*Very seriously*) Turn off the lights when you leave a room. (*Exits.*)

Dwight: We'd like to go out into our audience now and talk to some of you about your favorite "Dumb Dad Tricks." (*Carries mike with him; spots Girl 1.*) What's your favorite "Dumb Dad Trick"?

Girl 1: (*Stands.*) My dad likes to start his car after it's already started. It makes this really weird screeching noise. (*Sits.*)

Dwight: Ooh, that's a good one all right. (*To Guy 1, who stands*) How about you?

Guy 1: (*Stands.*) My favorite "Dumb Dad Trick" is when he forgets to take his coffee off the roof of the car before he takes off for work!

Dwight: I'll bet that's a real neighborhood show stopper all right! (*To Girl 2*) And you, young lady?

Girl 2: (*Stands.*) Dad really looks funny when he comes to church with those little pieces of toilet paper stuck to his face!

Dwight: Ah yes, Dad's 911 response to shaving while asleep! Well, that's all the time we have for this segment right now, folks, but we'll be right back with more fun after this commercial break.

Adman: (*Enters; presents as a dramatic narrative.*) We really got scared when Dad complained of chest pains. It was right after dinner when it hit him—a sharp, jabbing sensation right here. (*Pointing to chest area*) Dad has been under a lot of stress lately. The garage roof leaks. His license tags expired. His golf game was higher than his bowling score. And worst of all, Mom had beaten him to the crossword puzzle that evening. When he kept rubbing his chest, it was all we could do to keep calm. You can't imagine the relief we felt when we discovered the toothpick in Dad's shirt pocket. We learned a hard lesson that day. When your father asks for a toothpick...just say NO! (*Exits.*)

Dwight: Well we've had a good time poking fun at pa, but we all know that no Father's Day show would be complete without a little sentimental journey of sorts. So now we'd like to bring on three generations of the (*name of a real three-generation family in your congregation*) family. Saul, if you please.

(*Saul does a series of rim-shots. Son 2, Dad 4 and Dad 5 enter and cross to center.*)

Son 2: (*Looks at his dad. Singing his own made-up tune*)
    You are everything a pal should be,
    As a dad you've got the knack,
    It's easy to say, "I love you, Dad,"
    Because you give it back.

Dad 4: (*Looks at his dad. Also singing a made-up tune*)
    You are everything I want to be,
    As a friend, you've got the touch,
    Today my life is truly rich,
    Because, Dad, you gave so much.

Dad 5: (*Moves in between them both and puts his arms around their shoulders. Singing loudly yet another made-up tune*)
    I'm the one who's so enriched,

Among us there is a bond,
My dad, you see, gave me his love,
I merely passed it on.

(*They bow and exit, as Saul does a series of rim-shots while the applause tape plays.*)

Dwight: (*Dabbing at a tear*) Very nice. (*Sniffs.*) Thank you. Sentiment running amok all over this show, isn't it? Well, to wind up our tribute to fathers today, I'd like to ask all the fathers in our audience (*congregation*) to come down and stand along the front. Saul, a little traveling music, if you please.

(*Saul does his usual rim-shots until the fathers are down front.*)

Dwight: Earlier today we passed out song sheets to all the kids and moms in the audience, and now we're all going to sing a little song in honor of you dads. Ready, everyone?

(*Dwight cues everyone to start. The song can be sung to the tune of "M-O-T-H-E-R," sometimes known as "M Is for the Million Things She Gave Me."*)

F is for the fun he's given to me,
A is always allowing me to grow,
T is for his teaching me what's right from wrong,
H is holding my hand when I feel low—
E is for his endless sense of caring,
R is for his precious remote control,
Put them all together, they spell FATHER . . .
Faults and all, we love him so! (*Applause.*)

Dwight: Now all you moms, sons, and daughters—come down front and give your special guy a big Father's Day hug! Unclaimed fathers will be turned in to the lost and found! Happy Father's Day, everyone!

(*Applause tape plays, Saul gives a few rim-shots and provides some drum fill as all the actors come out from the wings and mingle with the fathers up front. For extra celebration, consider having a Father's-Day Fun and Fellowship time after the show.*)

THE END

THE F-A-T-H-E-R SONG

(This can be sung to the tune of "M-O-T-H-E-R," sometimes known as "M Is for the Million Things She Gave Me.")

F is for the fun he's given to me,

A is always allowing me to grow,

T is for his teaching me what's right from wrong,

H is holding my hand when I feel low—

E is for his endless sense of caring,

R is for his precious remote control,

Put them all together, they spell FATHER...
Faults and all, we love him so! (*Applause.*)

THE F-A-T-H-E-R SONG

(This can be sung to the tune of "M-O-T-H-E-R," sometimes known as "M Is for the Million Things She Gave Me.")

F is for the fun he's given to me,

A is always allowing me to grow,

T is for his teaching me what's right from wrong,

H is holding my hand when I feel low—

E is for his endless sense of caring,

R is for his precious remote control,

Put them all together, they spell FATHER...
Faults and all, we love him so! (*Applause.*)

SEASONINGS

BY PAUL NEALE LESSARD

....

"Give thanks whatever happens"

(1 Thessalonians 5:18).

THEME

Thanksgiving.

SUMMARY

As three teenagers prepare a turkey for the Thanksgiving meal, they come to an understanding of how God works in their lives.

CHARACTERS

Emily–The older sister, she is confident but a little too self-assured.

Aaron–The younger brother, he is somewhat sarcastic and not too happy about having to help out. (Emily and Aaron are only about a year apart.)

Andi–Emily and Aaron's cousin, she is unconventional but quite perceptive about life. Seventeen or 18, she's total energy, always moving, and intelligent. The crazier she dresses, the better the contrast between who we initially perceive her to be and who she really is.

SETTING

The play is set in a kitchen. There's a table center stage, and this is where the majority of the action takes place. An additional sideboard-style table and a stool are set to stage right and stage left, respectively. The center stage table has all the props necessary for the scene, including a bowl of water. On the table, directly in front of where Aaron will stand, should be a plastic bowl about the size of a cereal bowl. To Aaron's right, at the edge of the table, should be a small cup or unbreakable glass. Whether a real turkey and real ingredients are used is your call, but the use of a real turkey can greatly enhance the impact and humor of the play. Throughout the play, the actors are preparing the turkey and the stuffing. Even when the script does not note specific activity, all actors, especially Emily, should be working away, keeping their hands busy with something.

PROPS

Turkey roaster, turkey (or reasonable facsimile), kitchen towel, spices, measuring cups and spoons, two aprons, a recipe (card or piece of paper), three plastic bowls, dishrags, salt- and pepper shakers, box of salt, bread and bread knife, onions, bouillon cubes, portable radio with headphones, any other miscellaneous kitchen cooking items to dress the set. You'll also need appropriate stage lights and sound.

THE SCRIPT
"Seasonings"

(Scene opens with Emily entering. She's wearing an apron and carrying a large roaster. She sets it down on the table and takes the lid off.)

Emily: *(Looking at the recipe card and then around the table)* There are the bowls, the measuring cup... OK, I think I've got everything that Mom's recipe calls for. Let's see, *(looking at her watch)* we've got one hour to get this turkey ready for the oven. *(Yells offstage.)* Aaron, get your lazy body out of bed! I'm not doing all this work by myself. I seem to remember that you volunteered us to get the turkey ready and make the stuffing. *(She begins to organize all the various ingredients.)*

(Aaron enters with a severe case of "bedhead," or messed up hair. He's wearing an oversized T-shirt and hopelessly stretched-out sweat pants. It's obvious that he's just gotten out of bed. He's not moving very fast. He crosses to the end of the table and stands there, not looking at Emily.)

Emily: *(Sarcastic but not hurtful)* I love what you've done with your hair.

(He yawns, his eyes only half open.)

Emily: *(Gently needling him)* C'mon, cover your mouth when you yawn. *(She takes him by the shoulders and steers him in front of the turkey.)* I need your help, Aaron, we've got lots of work to do.

Aaron: *(Another yawn)* Hmm...

Emily: *(Back at work)* Did Andi get in last night?

Aaron: *(Staring down at the turkey, big sigh)* I don't have a good feeling about this.

Emily: *(Shoving the dishrag into Aaron's stomach for him to take)* No? Well, it's too late to back out now, Aaron; we've only got one hour to get this turkey ready to cook. So you wash this bird while I start making the stuffing. Did Andi get in last night?

Aaron: *(Another yawn)* Yeah, I picked her up at the airport at midnight. She said she would come down and help us this morning. *(He looks at Emily for the first time.)* I think Andi is going through another phase.

Emily: Yeah? Does that mean she's not dressing like a rock star anymore? *(Emily takes a slice of bread out of a bag and begins to cut it into cubes for stuffing. She notices that Aaron is just standing there.)* Hey, Mr. Morning, you're going to have to move your body to actually clean the turkey. First you need to reach inside and take out the little bag.

Aaron: (*Reaching inside the turkey*) Oh, this is gross! (*Under his breath*) I feel like a veterinarian. (*Pulling out a handful of "stuff"*) Ugh... (*To Emily*) What do I do with this... this... stuff?

Emily: (*Motioning, she's all business*) Put it into that bowl. Now wash the turkey inside and out with cold water. Let's see... (*Looks at recipe and continues cutting bread, putting it into a large bowl.*)

Aaron: (*Groaning again as he washes*) I don't have a good feeling about this, Emily.

Emily: (*Somewhat irritated*) Listen, you're the one who told Mom and Dad we could start preparing the Thanksgiving dinner while they picked up Grandma and Grandpa from the airport. (*Warningly, waving the bread knife in front of him*) It's too late to change your mind!

Aaron: No, I mean I don't have a good feeling about celebrating Thanksgiving this afternoon. After the year we've had, I don't think any of us are feeling very thankful.

Emily: (*Back to business*) Speak for yourself. I'm thankful.

Aaron: Yeah? Well, I guess you have a reason to be thankful now that your dry spell has finally ended and you've found another boyfriend.

Emily: Hey, I may have had a dry spell, but at least it wasn't a dating DROUGHT like you're having.

(*Emily notices Aaron has stopped working, looks at the recipe.*)

Emily: Now Mom's recipe says to drain and pat the turkey dry.

(*Aaron looks skeptical but grabs a towel, picks up the turkey, and dries it on his shoulder as if he's burping a baby. Emily is oblivious as she works on the stuffing.*)

Emily: (*Sarcastically*) So, you're saying that because YOU don't feel thankful, we shouldn't have this big Thanksgiving dinner like we always do, like every other person, everywhere else in the nation will be having today?

Aaron: (*Hurt by her sarcasm*) Emily, it just seems like dinner will be this big phony deal, just a show where we all pretend we're so happy and thankful but we're really not. (*Looks at his sister and sees she's not trying to understand.*) Oh, I don't know... What's next?

Emily: (*Holding up the saltshaker, which should be half-full*) Mom's recipe says to put in a quarter inch of salt. (*Turns to her brother and indicates with her thumb and index finger about a quarter of an inch apart. She hands him the saltshaker.*)

Aaron: (*Unsure, he takes the saltshaker.*) A quarter inch? Not a tablespoon or anything like that?

Emily: Yeah, a quarter of an inch. You know Mom's recipes; she just makes them up and writes them down. Put the salt inside the turkey as well as on the outside.

(Emily is once again oblivious to her brother as he salts the turkey.)

Aaron: *(Starts pouring the salt inside and then unscrews the top of the shaker and pours it all in. To himself)* That can't be more than an eighth of an inch; I'm gonna need more salt. *(He picks up the salt box and pours more inside.)* Are you sure Mom said to put in a quarter of an inch?

Emily: That's right.

Aaron: Seems like a lot of salt to me.

Emily: You'd better do what the recipe says, Aaron. You know Mom can be pretty particular about how she wants things done.

Aaron: OK, OK. A quarter of an inch on the outside, too?

Emily: Probably a quarter of an inch all together, inside and out. Just sprinkle it around. *(To herself)* Sheesh! How hard can it be?

Aaron: *(To himself)* Uh-oh, I might've put too much salt on the inside. Oh well, if I just put an eighth of an inch on the outside I should be fine. *(Pours the salt liberally on the top of the turkey to cover it with an eighth of an inch.)*

Emily: *(Looking at the recipe)* Two cups of chopped celery...

Aaron: It's just going to be a big show.

Emily: What is?

Aaron: Thanksgiving dinner.

Emily: *(Irritated)* Aaron, who made you the thankfulness police? Do you have to make sure everybody is truly thankful before we can eat turkey and cranberry sauce?

Aaron: *(Sharply)* I'm just saying we need to be honest. This hasn't been the best year for our family. *(Sarcastic, focusing attention on the turkey so he doesn't have to look into Emily's eyes)* Or were you happy when Dad got laid off his job? *(Handling turkey roughly)* Wrecking MY car may have been a thrill for you, but I don't particularly enjoy having to walk everywhere because we can't afford to fix it. And you have to admit that Mom's surgery scared us all. After that kind of year, I don't feel very thankful.

Emily: *(Equally sharp)* Then maybe you should skip Thanksgiving dinner and leave more turkey for us.

Aaron: *(Looking at the turkey)* It might be best to leave the turkey for you anyway...

Emily: *(Sighing, handing Aaron some onions)* Here, chop the onions. Aaron, even if you've had a bad year...

Aaron: *(Attempting to correct her)* We all have.

Emily: *(Not giving in)* Even if YOU'VE had a bad year, I still have plenty to be thankful for. So I'm eating turkey.

Aaron: *(Angrily)* Emily... *(He's interrupted by his cousin Andi, who bursts on to the stage dressed in grunge or whatever the latest fashion craze is. She's lis-*

tening to a portable radio with headphones and singing at the top of her lungs. Her hair should be as bizarre as possible. Andi should end up center stage behind the other two actors.)*

Andi: *(Singing along with the song on the radio)* "And I said if you don't leave me alone, I'll find someone that will. Don't come around here no more, no more, unless you'll pay my bills...Owww..."

(Andi goes into an extended air-guitar solo, making screeching noises at the top of her lungs. Emily and Aaron try to talk over her.)

Emily: *(Trying to be heard over the noise)* What's happened to Andi?

Aaron: *(Also trying to be heard)* I tried to warn you; she's into something new. I'm not sure what she's into, but I know it's not what she used to be into.

Emily: *(Trying to understand)* You mean she's not into that stuff she was into where she wore that other stuff and was into that hair thing?

Aaron: Yeah, she's not into that anymore. That's what she used to be into. Now she's into something else... *(Slightly confused)* I think that's what she's into.

(Emily turns and takes the headphones off of Andi's head.)

Emily: Andi, don't wake up the turkey.

Andi: *(Looking down at the turkey)* Cool. Are we really going to eat that?

Aaron: Emily will anyway.

Emily: *(Trying to shove a bouillon cube and a bowl into Andi's hands)* Here, Andi, mix this with a bowl of water.

Andi: *(Pulls back and in an outburst of energy twirls around.)* Notice anything different?

Emily: *(Caught off guard)* Uh, that's hard to say, Andi. What should we be looking for?

Andi: I'm totally free. I can do whatever I want now.

Emily: *(Somewhat impatiently)* What're you talking about?

Andi: *(Solemnly)* I've found the real me.

Aaron: Wow, I didn't know you were missing. Was your picture on a milk carton last month?

Andi: *(Thoughtfully)* Hmm, I don't think so.

Emily: You've found the real you? What's that supposed to mean?

Andi: *(Earnestly)* I can be forgetful and moody now. I can be happy one minute and sad the next. I don't have to talk to my parents again until I start college if I don't want to. No matter what I say or do, people will just roll their eyes and say, "Oh well, don't try to explain her; she's found her true self. That's just who she is."

Aaron: *(Playing along)* Sounds good to me! *(Feeling the effects of the onions, Aaron starts to rub his eyes.)*

Emily: I think I would keep looking if I were you, Andi.

Andi: I think this'll be my best Thanksgiving yet. Finally I have something to be thankful for.

> (*Aaron begins to sniffle, the onions are making him cry.*)

Andi: Aaron, what's wrong?

Aaron: It's these onions. They're making my eyes water.

Emily: If you let me take a picture of you with your eyes full of tears like that, I could show it around school and your dating drought would be over. (*Handing Andi the cube and bowl successfully this time*) Andi, dissolve this cube in the bowl of water. I need it for the stuffing.

Andi: Cool.

> (*They all resume working on the stuffing.*)

Andi: Are you sure you'll need that much onion? Seems like an awful lot.

Emily: That's what the recipe calls for.

Aaron: Yeah? Does it say we need an "inch" of onions?

Emily: No, (*reading the recipe*) Mom says we need the measuring cup full.

Aaron: (*Not noticing the cup, picks up the bowl. To himself*) This looks more like a bowl to me. Oh well…(*He puts all the chopped onions in the bowl and then pours them into the large bowl that Emily is making the stuffing in.*)

Aaron: I still don't have a good feeling about this.

Andi: About what?

Emily: (*Annoyed*) Aaron thinks we'll be hypocrites by having a big Thanksgiving meal because we really don't have anything to be thankful for this year.

Andi: You don't have anything to be thankful for?

Aaron: Of course I have things to be thankful for. It's just that we've had some tough times this year. I think to pretend you're thankful when it's been a lousy year is pretty phony.

Andi: (*Stopping to eat some of the bread Emily has cut up*) So, are you saying you can be thankful only for the good things that happen to you?

Aaron: (*Stupid look on his face, mocking his cousin*) Duh, I guess so.

Andi: What if good things come out of the tough times you've had?

Emily: (*Smelling blood*) Whoa, look out, Aaron. She's going to tell you that your dating drought will be for the best because when you finally get another girl to go out with you, you'll appreciate her more. (*Wickedly*) That's assuming you actually get another date in this life.

Aaron: (*Somewhat irritated, rubbing his eyes from the onions*) Andi, are you telling me I should be thankful for the rough times our family has had this past year?

Andi: (*She steps back from the table and does a twirl. As she questions her cousin she doesn't actually look at him.*) Maybe.

Aaron: (*Mimicking her*) Yeah, well, cool.

Andi: (*Ignoring him*) Aaron, do you like stuffing?

Emily: (*Laughing*) He loves stuffing; that's why Mom's recipe calls for an ice-cream pail full of bread crumbs.

Aaron: Sure, I like to eat stuffing. So what?

Andi: (*Stretching, as if she's getting ready for an athletic event*) Would you ever eat a whole onion?

Aaron: (*Growing more irritated*) Of course not. My dating drought would become a dating desert.

Andi: But you like onions when they're a part of something else you're eating?

Aaron: Yeah, I suppose so.

Andi: Like stuffing.

Aaron: (*Losing patience*) Yes, Andi, I like onions in my stuffing. I also like green eggs and ham. So what?

Andi: (*She stops moving, picks up a spice bottle, and plays with it as she talks.*) Would you say that a little bit of onion makes the stuffing better?

Aaron: (*Fully exasperated*) Does it matter?

Emily: (*The light dawns.*) Onions on their own might be too strong to eat, but a little bit of onion, when mixed in with the other ingredients, can add spice to whatever you're making.

Andi: (*Back to stretching again*) Yes, that's what I'm saying.

Aaron: (*To himself*) The amount of onion I've got here is going to add more than just a little flavor. I know that already!

Andi: Some of the spices in your stuffing are things you wouldn't want to eat on their own. They'd be too bitter or hot. But when they're mixed with all the other ingredients from the recipe, they make the stuffing taste better.

Aaron: (*Sarcastic, but unclear*) Cool, so, uh, what's the deal here?

Emily: The deal is that you can eat the Thanksgiving meal with a clear conscience if you can be thankful for the tough times we've had this past year.

Andi: Because the tough times can bring good things.

Aaron: Great! Does this mean I'm going to have more luck getting a date?

Andi: (*Trying to be positive*) Maybe.

Emily: (*Trying to hold back, but unable to resist*) Actually, it means that because you can't get a date right now, a lot of girls are living better lives.

Andi: (*Giggling in spite of herself*) Emily—cool—I never thought of it that way. (*Sees Aaron.*) Sorry, Aaron.

  (*The two girls laugh. Aaron gives them dirty looks.*)

Emily: (*All business again*) This stuffing is about ready (*looks at her watch*) and the turkey should go into the oven right now. (*She gives the turkey a good look for the first time since Aaron began to work on it and is horrified.*)

Aaron, what happened to the turkey? (*Sees the overwhelming amount of onions in the bowl.*) And why did you put so much onion in the stuffing?

Aaron: Emily, Emily, don't worry. You heard Andi; these things can work out for the best.

Andi: (*Standing still for a moment*) I said that?

Aaron: Well, something like that.

Andi: (*Moving again*) Cool.

    (*Lights fade.*)

THE END

ANGELS WE HAVE HEARD ON HIGH

BY JIM OLLHOFF

....

"Whoever wants to be the most important must be last of all and servant of all"
(MARK 9:35b).

THEME

Christmas/Advent.

SUMMARY

Ralph, a rookie guardian angel, learns the value of serving in humble ways.

CHARACTERS

Ralph–A naive rookie angel, he is currently overworked and fighting a cold.

Maximus–Upwardly mobile angel.

Dionysus–Upwardly mobile angel.

Parcellian–A slightly grumpy middle-management angel.

Artemon–A nervous angel.

Gabriel–The chief angel, he is in charge of all the angel assignments.

SETTING

Angel workroom. The workroom is a cluttered mess. Several desks or tables fill the room. Each one is stacked with thick file folders. In a couple of places the stacks have tipped, leaving loose papers on the table and papers spilled on the floor. Bookshelves and file cabinets stand along the back wall. A computer terminal sits on one or more desks in the back. An open briefcase sits on a desk in front and several notebooks litter the scene. All in all, the scene looks like several people have been far too busy to keep it clean.

PROPS

File folders stuffed with paper, a glass of water, a handkerchief, two briefcases, a backpack, two stacks of envelopes rubber banded together (one stack with the "angel assignments" in them), and various office supplies for background material (such as pens, pencils, staples, paper clips, and so on.)

THE SCRIPT
"Angels We Have Heard on High"

(Lights come up to find Ralph sitting quietly at one of the front desks. He is writing feverishly, concentrating solely on his work. Ralph squints through his thick, horn-rimmed glasses. He is dressed like the stereotypical nerd—wearing a suit and bow tie that don't really match. Half of his shirt is

untucked, and he may have a calculator in his pocket. His hair stands up on one side, and a large, white hankie sits crumpled to his left.

After a moment, Ralph grabs the hankie and catches a violent sneeze, then continues working on his paper. He squeezes the skin between his eyes, trying to wring out a headache. He honks his nose, clears his throat, and sniffs. Ralph is a picture of a cold sufferer that's almost painful to watch. Ralph reaches for his glass of water, misses and knocks the glass over, spilling the water on several files and some computer paper.)

Ralph: Oh, rats! *(He jumps to wipe it up but manages to knock the whole stack of files onto the floor.)*

Ralph: Aauugghh!

(He glances to see if anyone is in the room and kneels under the desk to rescue the files. Enter Maximus and Dionysus from stage left. They are smartly dressed in business suits and carry expensive-looking briefcases. They are the picture of what angels would look like if they were all Ivy League graduates rising up the angel corporate ladder.)

Maximus: Hello?

(Ralph, on hearing Maximus, jerks his head up and bangs it on the desk.)

Ralph: Ouch!

Dionysus: Hey, Ralph, you all right?

(Ralph gets up, rubbing his head with one hand, and precariously balancing the files in the other.)

Ralph: Hi, guys. How you doing?

Maximus: All right. Busier than ever.

(Maximus and Dionysus go right to a table and start looking through and rearranging files.)

Dionysus: Ralph, you look a bit . . . shall we say, neatness-challenged today.

Maximus: Yeah, more than usual.

Ralph: Didn't sleep last night. I was on assignment. Just filling out the report now. Is being an angel always this busy?

Dionysus: You know, I've been on the guardian shift for 2,500 years, and it has never been as busy as this.

Maximus: Yeah, something's going on. Maybe it's another drill.

Dionysus: So, Ralph, where was your assignment last night?

Ralph: A farmer in Samaria—one of his cows got lost. I had to make sure it didn't fall into the river. *(Ralph blows his nose again.)*

Maximus: Sounds like you caught a cold.

Ralph: Got it when I fell into the river. *(Ralph snorts again and then stuffs the hankie into his pocket.)*

Maximus: I'm so glad I don't have animal duty anymore. I haven't had to save a dog or cat in over a thousand years. *(Maximus looks at Ralph and* *suddenly realizes he said the wrong thing.)* Not that there's anything wrong with that, of course.

Dionysus: No, boy, if we didn't save those cows, then...then a... *(Dionysus searches in vain for a suitable end to the sentence, finally shrugs his shoulders, and returns to looking through a folder.)*

Maximus: Animal duty is fine work for a rookie angel.

Dionysus: That's right. You gotta work your way up—pay your dues before you get to where we are.

Ralph: What did you do last night?

(Dionysus and Maximus don't mean to be cocky, but they are, after all, very proud of their recent activities.)

Dionysus: I kept the High Priest of Jerusalem safe from a bout of salmonella. Bad fish.

Maximus: I kept a war from starting between the Romans and the Parthian tribes.

(Ralph sneezes again. Good and depressed now, Ralph starts putting his files into a backpack. Dionysus and Maximus approach him, trying to be helpful.)

Maximus: You know, Ralph, maybe there are some things you could do to get more important work.

Dionysus: So you don't have to guard animals forever. *(Waves his hand in front of his face as if to indicate that Ralph smells like a cow.)*

Ralph: Yeah? Like what?

Maximus: Well, you could dress a little more professionally.

Ralph: *(Ralph looks down at his own clothes.)* What, this still isn't right? I spent 25 minutes picking out this outfit.

Maximus: And your backpack...why not try getting a nice briefcase? Sure, I paid big money for this, but it helped to get me where I am today.

Ralph: An expensive briefcase helped you serve God better?

Maximus: Well...uh...you gotta look the part.

(Enter Parcellian. He is older than the rest and better dressed. Hurried and preoccupied, he makes a beeline for the open briefcase.)

Dionysus: Hi, Parcellian.

Maximus: *(Nodding his greeting)* Parcellian.

Ralph: How you doin'?

Parcellian: Hi, guys. Busy, busy, busy.

(The others realize that they have spent enough time shooting the breeze, so they get back to work, too.)

Dionysus: Have you heard why we're so busy lately?

Parcellian: No, but rumor is that we're all gonna be starting double duty tonight.

(The others are visibly disappointed at the news.)

Maximus: Something's going on.

Dionysus: The Master's got something going that's bigger than anything he's done before.

Parcellian: No doubt. I already had two assignments this morning.

Ralph: What did you do?

Parcellian: Well, my first assignment was to prevent an earthquake that would've damaged the temple in Jerusalem.

Ralph: Really?

Parcellian: And then I had to put a new star in the sky. What did you do?
 (*Ralph locks his eyes on the floor, fidgeting nervously.*)

Ralph: Um, a cow...had a problem...I helped it.

Parcellian: As busy as we are, and you helped a cow?
 (*There is an extraordinarily painful silence. Maximus, who has been working on his papers, tries to rescue Ralph.*)

Maximus: Well, it WAS his assignment...

Parcellian: What did you do the day before yesterday?

Ralph: Ummm...

Parcellian: Well?

Ralph: Well, there was this sheep lost on the edge of this cliff. The owners couldn't find it, and the sheep was scared stiff, you see...

Parcellian: Never mind.

Dionysus: We were suggesting to Ralph that maybe he could work himself up out of animal duty.

Parcellian: Well, I guess someone has to do those kinds of assignments.

Maximus: We thought maybe if he got a tie that matched, or combed his hair, or got a nice briefcase...

Dionysus: Or all three...

Maximus: That he could maybe get a nice human assignment.

Ralph: Yeah, but I really don't mind doing animal duty.

Parcellian: What?

Ralph: I mean, I'm happy to serve the Father, even if it's in the little things.

Parcellian: Well, it's no wonder you've never been promoted.

Maximus: Don't you have any ambition, Ralph?

Parcellian: Please, Maximus. I'll handle this. (*Parcellian goes over to Ralph, and puts his arm around him, like an older brother who is mentoring the silly, naive, inexperienced sibling.*)

Parcellian: You gotta understand something about angel-ing.

Ralph: What?

Parcellian: Nothing like it. Nowhere. Being an angel, well, it's like working for the Mighty One himself.

Ralph: It IS working for the Mighty One himself.

Parcellian: That's just it. The MIGHTY one. Being an angel is doing mighty acts for the Mighty God.

(*Maximus and Dionysus think this is really neat, and they write down what Parcellian just said. Ralph is respectful but unimpressed.*)

Parcellian: Yeah, I like that. Doing mighty acts for the Mighty God.

Ralph: Mmm.

(*Parcellian loses himself in his own philosophy. He starts speaking rhythmically.*)

Parcellian: You gotta climb every mountain. Ford every stream. Dream the impossible dream...

Ralph: You're not gonna break into song, are you?

Parcellian: You gotta WANT to do mighty acts, Ralph. Only mighty acts are deserving of a mighty God.

Ralph: Saving a sheep isn't a mighty act?

Parcellian: You're missing the point here. Something big is going on these days. Something huge. This might be the time when you could rise to do something fantastic. This could be your time. What do you think?

Ralph: Last week I saved an African wildebeest.

(*They all give up and go back to their work.*)

Ralph: No really, this wildebeest was up on this high cliff...

Parcellian: Sorry, Ralph, but we're really busy.

(*Ralph gets the message and sits down at his chair to work again. After a moment of silence*)

Ralph: They're also called gnus, you know.

All: Ralph!

(*He shuts up again. They all work quietly. Then the angel Artemon bursts in. He's breathing heavily, as if he's run all the way. He's as white as a sheet.*)

Maximus: Artemon! What's wrong?

Artemon: Oh, my...

Dionysus: Are you all right?

Artemon: You'll never guess what I just heard.

Parcellian: You heard something? What? What?

Artemon: My partner's cousin has an uncle whose best friend's brother works in the same office as Gabriel.

Dionysus: Gabriel?

Parcellian: You mean, THE Gabriel?

Artemon: (*Artemon nods in somber confirmation.*) The big kahuna.

Maximus: So, what'd he say?

Artemon: You gotta promise not to say anything to anybody.

(*They all ad-lib their solemn promises.*)

Artemon: My partner's cousin's uncle's best friend's brother overheard Gabriel speaking about...

Parcellian: What? Speaking about what?

Artemon: The Messiah. Jesus is going to earth.

(They can't contain their awe at the magnitude of this news. They are instantly on their feet.)

Parcellian: What do you mean?

Dionysus: How's he going?

Maximus: Is he going to parade out of the sky?

Ralph: Is he taking any animals with him?

Artemon: *(Artemon puts up his hands as if to say, "That's all I know.")* That's all I know.

Parcellian: You come in here with news like that, and that's all you know?

Artemon: I just call 'em like I hear 'em.

Ralph: Incredible.

Maximus: That would explain all the extra work lately.

Parcellian: I bet Jesus goes down to earth on a fiery chariot, with all of us out in front blowing our trumpets.

Maximus: He'll be crowned king instantly. Ha! And they thought King David was something. They haven't seen anything yet. Talk about strength and power... whew!

Dionysus: He'll be the greatest king ever on earth.

Maximus: The leader the humans need.

Parcellian: When he speaks, nations will quiver.

Maximus: Kings will whimper.

Dionysus: With a sword in one hand and the Father's word in the other.

Parcellian: He will undo the unrighteous, crush the criminals, punish the perpetrators, disable the desperadoes... *(He's working really hard on this now.)* Wail on the wicked... bruise the... bad people, discipline the... dunderheads.

Ralph: But didn't Isaiah say something about a suffering servant?

Maximus: It just so happens I was speaking to Isaiah the other day, and...

Parcellian: *(Cutting off Maximus)* What do you mean, Ralph?

Ralph: Well, this is just a thought, you know, but what if Jesus went in like, say... a servant?

Parcellian: Don't be ridiculous!

Artemon: Come on.

Dionysus: Why on earth would he do that?

Ralph: I don't know, just a thought.

Maximus: Artemon, did you hear anything else?

Artemon: No, just that.

(No one is quite sure what to do now.)

Dionysus: I say we send Artemon over to the central office to see if there's any more news.

Parcellian: Good idea!

Maximus: Yeah, let's do that. We'll cover for you. OK with you, Artemon?

Artemon: (*With new determination*) OK, I'll do it.

(*An air of intense, pompous grandness washes over the room, as if the angels were sending Artemon off to war.*)

Artemon: I promise, on my honor as an angel, I won't come back until I know something.

Maximus: Good luck, brave Artemon.

(*All except Artemon put their hands over their hearts and start humming the Green Berets song—or some other patriotic, military song—and Artemon bravely steps off stage left. They watch him go, and then a moment later, Artemon explodes back into the room.*)

Artemon: Gabriel's coming! Gabriel's coming!

(*The five angels are terrified at being caught loafing on the job. With arms and legs moving wildly, they frantically jump into their seats and make it look like they are hard at work. They have sat only a moment when Gabriel enters. They pretend not to notice. Gabriel is carrying a large bundle of envelopes in one hand and a smaller bundle of five envelopes in the other hand.*)

Gabriel: Hard at work, gentlemen?

(*Their heads pop up, and with forced surprise they get up to greet Gabriel.*)

All: Hello, what a surprise. Good to meet you. Hello, Gabriel.

(*They all reach to shake his hand.*)

Maximus: What a great honor it is to meet you, sir. A great honor. Great honor.

Dionysus: Hello, sir. I'm Dionysus, one of your biggest fans.

Parcellian: Hello, Gabriel. We met 10 years ago at the Heaven Hoedown Dance.

(*Gabriel doesn't remember but tries to be nice about it anyway.*)

Gabriel: Oh, really.

Artemon: What a great honor and surprise to have someone of your magnitude and greatness here among us.

Ralph: Hi, I'm Ralph.

(*Ralph trips over a chair and crashes to the floor. They help him up. Gabriel puts his larger stack of envelopes on the nearest table so he can give Ralph a hand.*)

Ralph: I'm OK, I'm OK.

Parcellian: So, Gabriel, to what do we owe the honor of this visit for which we are so grateful and excited about?

Gabriel: Well, I suppose you're all wondering why there's been so much extra work lately.

(*All except Ralph immediately deny wondering.*)

All: No, never, no.

Gabriel: I have some exciting news. Jesus is going to earth to save the humans.

(*They are awe-struck and giddy with excitement.*)

Dionysus: That's great!

Maximus: Fantastic!

Ralph: Wow!

Gabriel: Yes, it's exciting. Jesus will be born in the town of...

Parcellian: (*Interrupting Gabriel*) Uh, excuse me, um, sir? I thought you said he'd be BORN. (*Laughs nervously.*)

Gabriel: Yes.

Parcellian: You mean, he's not going to go in a fantastic parade, with trumpets and fiery chariots?

Gabriel: Ummm, no.

Dionysus: Ahhh, so he'll be born into a rich and powerful family on earth.

Gabriel: Not really, no.

Maximus: (*Confused*) Then what?

Gabriel: Tell you what. Rather than explain it all now, we're going to explain it later to the entire group of angels. You'll get the full story then. For now, here are your assignments. (*Gabriel takes the rubber band off the small bundle of envelopes and hands an envelope to each of them.*) Take care on these assignments. This is a night the world will remember forever.

(*Gabriel leaves, forgetting his larger stack of envelopes on the table. The angels all are awe-struck and speechless. Slowly and reverently, they open their envelopes. They can hardly contain their emotion. Their voices tremble.*)

Dionysus: I'm to accompany three wise men to the place of Jesus' birth.

Artemon: Me, too. (*He and Dionysus exchange high fives.*)

Parcellian: I'm to visibly appear to a bunch of shepherds and tell them about the Messiah... I've never appeared visibly before.

Maximus: I appear with you, Parcellian. I'm to be part of an angelic chorus that says, "Give glory to God in heaven, and on earth let there be peace among the people who please God."

(*Ralph has read his assignment and put it back in the envelope.*)

Maximus: Ralph, what's your assignment?

Ralph: Animal duty. Again. (*Ralph was honestly hoping for more this time.*)

Parcellian: I'm sorry, Ralph.

Ralph: Biggest night of all time, and I'm taking care of animals.

Maximus: We'll tell you all about it, Ralph.

Dionysus: Yeah, not to worry.

Artemon: Well, I'd best be going. I've got to iron my brightest outfit.

Dionysus: Yeah, and I've got to make travel arrangements.

(*Artemon and Dionysus exit. Parcellian and Maximus follow them out.*)

Maximus: (*To Parcellian, as they exit*) Do you think we should sing this or get the trumpets out?

(*Everyone is gone now except Ralph, who's sitting next to the table and feeling lonely. After a moment, Gabriel enters and retrieves the envelopes he left behind. He starts to leave, but then sees Ralph and stops.)*

Gabriel: Ralph, you all right?

Ralph: Oh, hi. Yeah, fine. Just, well *(waving his assignment envelope)* I was kinda hoping for more.

Gabriel: More?

Ralph: I guess I wanted to be in the chorus with the other guys. Or a parade or something. Will there ever be a parade?

Gabriel: Oh, about 33 years from now there will be a parade, of sorts, to a hill outside Jerusalem.

Ralph: *(Sighing)* I guess I'm a bit jealous of the other guys always getting the big assignments.

Gabriel: *(Gabriel sits down next to him.)* You know, the Master has a peculiar way of doing things. Greatness is measured by how you serve, not by how stupendous your acts are.

Ralph: But the other guys are doing such... well, BIG things.

Gabriel: *(Smiling)* You'd be surprised at how often the Master is found in the little things, even the humble and sometimes forgotten things.

Ralph: Like the animal duty?

Gabriel: *(Giving Ralph a reassuring pat on the back)* Yeah. In the animal duty.

Ralph: Thanks, Gabriel.

  (Ralph smiles, feeling a bit better. Gabriel gets up to leave. Ralph quickly takes out his paper.)

Ralph: Hey, Gabriel. Can you tell me how to get to Bethlehem? I have to calm some animals in a stable—apparently a baby is to be born there tonight.

Gabriel: Sure. Take a left outside the pearly gates, and...

  (Lights fade as Gabriel leans over and starts pointing out directions to Bethlehem.)

THE END

MARK AND HAROLD'S ANGEL SWING

BY RICH MELHEIM

....

"God sent the angel Gabriel to Nazareth, a town in Galilee, to a virgin . . . Her name was Mary" **(LUKE 1:26b, 27b).**

THEME
Christmas.

SUMMARY
Amidst the hectic preparations for a Sunday school Christmas program, one little angel helps the leaders refocus on the reason for the season.

CHARACTERS
Noel–Noel is an uptight high school girl who has just inherited the honor of producing the elementary Sunday school pageant. She needs a strong singing voice and should wear glasses.

Gloria–Noel's reluctant helper, she needs to be able to play piano and should play accompaniment each time a song is sung.

Mark–A mischievous friend of Noel, he likes to give the girls a difficult time.

Harold–Mark's sidekick, he is rarely serious about anything.

Angel–He or she is an elementary-age student who doesn't mind being swung from the ceiling during the play. (**Director's Note:** Script is written as if a girl plays the angel. Change gender references if the part is played by a boy.)

Mary–An elementary-age girl playing the mother of Jesus.

Joseph–An elementary-age boy playing Mary's husband.

Artist–An elementary-age student who is to make the set.

Herod–An elementary-age student who is to play the king.

Assorted characters including—Two-person donkey, three wise ones (two girls and one boy), assorted angels, and assorted shepherds.

SETTING
The play is set in the sanctuary. The audience is a part of the play, so access should be fairly easy from the platform to the aisles. The set can be as elaborate as a beautiful Nativity scene or as simple as a couple of chairs around a milk-crate manger. A rope and pulley strong enough to hoist a small actress will be needed up front.

PROPS
Rope, block and tackle, wooden sheep on wheels or plush toy sheep, and a doll for baby Jesus. Costumes are at the director's discretion. Kids can be in bathrobes with towels on their heads or in Palestinian head-dresses and silken robes depending on the mood you wish to create. The only completely finished costumes required are an angel costume for the angel who is harnessed and flown slightly upside down onto the scene and a two-person donkey costume that can fall apart. You'll need appropriate stage lights and sound.

(**Director's Note:** The music is all congregational singing of traditional public domain songs. Directors can choose how many verses of each to sing. Songs include "O Come, All Ye Faithful"; "O Come, O Come, Emmanuel"; "O Little Town of Bethlehem"; "Away in a Manger"; "Angels We Have Heard on High"; "We Three Kings"; "Silent Night! Holy Night!"; and "Joy to the World." Since the audience becomes the "class," everyone is encouraged to sing.)

THE SCRIPT
"Mark and Harold's Angel Swing"

(Lights come up to find Noel pacing back and forth across the stage.)

Noel: *(Shouting as Gloria enters from rear)* Gloria! Gloria! Where have you been?

Gloria: You yelling at me?

Noel: We're in deep trouble, kid. Deep trouble.

Gloria: What are you talking about?

Noel: Remember when we said we'd help with the children's Christmas program?

Gloria: Yeah?

Noel: Well, suddenly Mrs. Fletcher is out of commission, and we're left in charge of the whole thing. The whole thing!

Gloria: What are you saying?

Noel: Your "buddies" Mark and Harold were hanging ropes here in the sanctuary to help float the angels in...

Gloria: *(Pointing to the rafters)* You let Mark and Harold climb up there with ropes?

Noel: Yeah! They said they wanted to help.

Gloria: Help? Mark and Harold? *(Rolling her eyes)* What happened?

Noel: They built an angel swing so it looked like the angel was actually flying.

Gloria: So, what happened after that?

Noel: Emergency room, that's what happened!

Gloria: They're in the hospital?

Noel: No, not them. Mrs. Fletcher, the Sunday school superintendent. She's the one in the hospital.

Gloria: What happened?

Noel: They sort of dropped something—or rather someone—on her, and now suddenly you and I are left to pull off this whole program.

Gloria: Just remembered. Gotta go change the air in my tires. Good luck, Noel. (*Starts to leave.*)

Noel: You gotta help me!

Gloria: Me? (Mimicking "Gone With the Wind") I don't know nothing about birthin' no Christmas programs, Miss Scarlet. Besides, I distinctly hear God calling me to be a missionary to Hawaii.

Noel: (*Restraining her friend*) Not so fast, Gloria. You're the one who suggested Mark and Harold in the first place. You owe me. (*Sees Mark and Harold approach with rope and block and tackle.*) Here come the masters of disaster now.

(*Mark and Harold enter singing to the tune of "Hark! the Herald Angels Sing" at the top of their lungs and acting proud of their feat.*)

Mark and Harold: Mark and Harold's angel swing
Lifted Fletcher on her wing!
Dropped an angel from the air,
Sent her to intensive care!
Now she lays, not feeling keen,
Send your flow'rs to 214!
In the hospital she lies,
Hoist the next one to the skies!
Mark and Harold's angel swing...

Noel: Cut! Cut! QUIET! This is not funny!

Mark: Funny? Did she say it's not funny?

Harold: I think it's funny. Do you think it's funny?

Gloria: (*Shrugging her shoulders*) I think it's funny.

Noel: Arrrgh! This is the only rehearsal we're going to have before the program, and since you two are the ones who messed this up for everyone, I'm putting you in charge with me. Mark, you're now the narrator.

Mark: Me?

Noel: Yes. You can't hurt anyone if all you do is read. Harold, you cue the actors. And Gloria, you play the piano for the carols. Mrs. Fletcher won't have use of her arms until after the casts come off.

Gloria: Are you sure the angel ropes are safe now?

Mark: We tested them after the little mishap. Everything is in A-1 condition.

Noel: Are you sure?

Harold: I'd bet your life on it.

Gloria: We should probably test them first just to see...

Noel: No time for that now. Here come the kids. Get to the piano, Gloria, and start with "O Come, All Ye Faithful." Places! Places, everyone! (*All characters enter singing "O Come, All Ye Faithful" with Gloria playing accompaniment.*)

Noel: (*After everyone is in*) Cut, cut, cut! Gloria! Gloria! Cut!

Harold: What a grouch!

Noel: I said cut! You kids have it all wrong! Gracefully! You must walk in gracefully. We are never going to get this program ready for Christmas if you don't pay a little more attention to what is going on. Narrator Mark, please read the opening lines as soon as everyone is in place up front.

Angel: (*Approaching Noel and tugging on her sleeve*) Noel? Noel?

Mark and Harold: (*Beginning to sing their satiric song at the top of their lungs to the tune of "The First Noel"*)

> The worst Noel, the angels did say
>
> was the one put in charge of the program today...
>
> (*Noel glares at Mark and Harold, shutting them up.*)

Noel: What is it, Angel?

Angel: I don't think I can go through with this.

Noel: It'll be fine. You make a darling angel.

Angel: But I don't think that this angel harness will work.

Noel: It'll be fine. I've been assured that everything is taken care of. Now, let's get going. We've only got this one rehearsal left.

Angel: Are you sure it will work now?

Noel: (*Hurrying her along*) It'll be fine. Just fine. Now run along and get ready for your lines.

Angel: But what if it doesn't work?

Noel: Whatever happens, just do your lines as you remember them. The show must go on!

Angel: But I've been looking at this, and I don't think it will...

Noel: Be a little angel, Angel, and run along now. Everything will be fine. And remember, whatever happens, just keep doing your lines. OK, everyone sit down except Mary. Mary! (*Looking frantically around the stage*) Harold, can you get Mary ready for her cue? (*Pauses.*) OK, now, action! Mark!

Mark: In the days of Herod the king, the angel Gabriel was sent from God unto a town named Nazareth, to a virgin disposed to a man named Joseph.

Noel: It's not disposed, Mark. It's espoused. Espoused!

Mark: Exposed?

Noel: Es-spoused. It means engaged.

Mark: Well, why didn't God just say that then?

Noel: In the King James Version...oh, never mind. Just read on. Read on!

Mark: To a virgin ex-spoused to a man named Joseph. And the virgin's name was Harry.

Noel: Mary!

> (*Harold quickly pushes Mary out.*)

Mary: What?

Noel: I'm not talking to you. Sit down.

Mary: But you called my name.

Noel: No. I was talking to Mark.

Mary: Then why did you call my name?

Noel: Never mind. Mark, the name was Mary!

Mark: But it looks like an H on my copy. It's Harry. You made a mistake.

Noel: *(Grabbing his script)* I did not. Give me that. *(Looking at the script, then with embarrassment)* Oh. *(After a long pause)* I guess I did. OK, so I made a mistake.

    (Kids giggle at each other.)

Noel: Even grown-ups are allowed to make a few mistakes now and then. Let's get on with it. Her name was Mary. Change it, Mark. The angel's name was Mary.

Mark: But...

Noel: No buts! Let's get going! *(Glancing at her watch)* Write it in, Mark. The angel's name was Mary. Let's go.

Mark: But Noel, the angel's name was...

Noel: *(Snappy)* Do what I tell you!

Mark: *(Raising his eyebrows)* All right, if you say so: In the days of Herod the king, the angel Mary was sent from God.

Noel: Wait! It's Gabriel! The angel Gabriel!

Mark: But you told me...

Noel: Never mind what I told you. Just do what I tell you! *(Flustered and looking at her watch)* Let's...uh...skip over this part. Go right to the song. Gloria? The song. *(Speaking to the audience as if they were all in her class)* Please excuse me. All this Christmas preparation gets on my nerves a little. I just want this to be...well, you know...a great program and, oh...

Harold: *(In all seriousness)* What she means to say is, she just wants this to be a meaningful Christmas experience for all who come to see it in order to honor the true spirit of Christmas.

    (Noel nods.)

Harold: And if she has to bash a few heads to do it, so be it!

Noel: *(Glaring and muttering under her breath)* I'll deal with you later. *(To the audience)* OK, kids. Chins up. Let's all sing! *(Doing a double take, surprised to see the sanctuary filled)* Wow, this is a big Sunday school class! They didn't tell me that I was going to have to rehearse with a class this large. *(Picking out someone in the front row)* You'd better behave, young man *(or lady)*, or I'm out of here, and you'll be stuck with Pastor *(fill in name of your pastor)* to finish the program. How would you like that? OK, kids, sing!

    (Noel leads the audience in singing "O Come, O Come, Emmanuel," while Gloria plays accompaniment on the piano.)

Noel: *(Looking at the audience)* Some of you must be new kids. I don't think I've met all of you before.

(Walks out into the audience with Harold and finds the tallest person in the crowd.)

Noel: You weren't singing, young man. Stand up please. *(At this point Noel needs to play with the audience. Make the person stand.)*

Harold: Boy, these sixth-graders are getting bigger every year.

Noel: What's your name? *(Waits for response.)* How old are you, anyway? *(Waits for response.)*

Harold: Must have flunked a few grades.

Noel: Oh, well, glad to have you here, *(fill in name).*

Harold: You want a bigger part in this show? *(Waits for response.)*

　　(If audience member says yes, **Harold says:** You got any money? *Pause, then Noel, embarrassed, pulls Harold back to the stage.)*

　　(If audience member says no, **Harold says:** Too bad, kid, I coulda made you a star. *Then Harold and Noel return to the stage.)*

Noel: Narrator, keep reading.

Artist: Miss Director, ma'am. Could you OK my sketches for the set so I can get the other kids painting?

Noel: Can't this wait? We're rehearsing.

Artist: They're waiting with the paint right now. It'll only take a minute.

Noel: OK. I'll take a look. Narrator Mark, read on! *(She puts on glasses and sits down to look at designs, oblivious to the action behind her. Harold swings Angel in on the rope harness.)*

Mark: And the Angel said...

Angel: *(Floating in upside down on the poorly designed harness, she crashes directly into Mary.)* Thou shalt...bring forth a son...and shalt call his name Jesus. He shall be called the Son of the Highest...and of his kingdom...there shall be...no...end.

Mark: And Mary said...

Mary: *(Pushing the Angel away)* Get her away from me!

Noel: *(Not looking up)* Stick to the script, Mary.

Mary: Behold, I am the handmaid of the Lord.

Mark: And the angel departed from her.

Noel: *(Without looking up from the set sketches)* That's fine, Angel, but try not to be so choppy next time.

Angel: Miss Director, ma'am. I don't think this is working.

Noel: That's my decision to make. On with the show.

　　(Angel is pulled out, still upside down. Joseph and Donkey join Mary for the journey.)

Mark: It came to pass that there went out a decree that all the world should be taxed, everyone in his own city. And Joseph went up from Nazareth to the city called Bethlehem, to be taxed with Mary, his wife, being great with child.

Harold: Noel?

Noel: What?

Harold: How did they know she was great with child? She hadn't even had one yet.

Noel: Well, they, uh...she...um...never mind. Next song, Gloria! (*To the audience*) Everyone, sing!

    (*Noel leads the audience in singing "O Little Town of Bethlehem," while Gloria plays accompaniment on the piano.*)

Mark: Should I go on?

Noel: Please go on.

Mark: And she brought forth her firstborn son, wrapped him in swaddling clothes, and laid him in a manger because there was no room for them in the inn.

Harold: They laid him in a cow feeder? Hey, Noel, is that really true?

Noel: Yes. Now can we please continue?

    (*Mary pulls out a doll from under her shawl and drops it head first in the manger.*)

Harold: Yo! Easy with the baby! They have soft heads, you know.

Noel: (*To Harold*) Is that what your brother did to you when you were a baby?

Harold: (*Sarcastically*) Funny. (*Thinking*) Actually, it was my sister.

Noel: (*To the audience*) Next song: "Away in a Manger." Ready, everyone?

    (*Noel starts the audience singing the song while Gloria plays accompaniment on the piano. During this song, Noel and Harold walk through the audience, encouraging everyone to sing. At the same time, assorted shepherds appear on the far side of the stage. Angel prepares to swing in again.*)

Angel: Miss Teacher person, ma'am. I honestly don't think this is working.

Noel: (*Watching shepherds, not seeing Angel*) Look, Angel, I'm the director here. I'll be the judge of that.

Artist: Teacher, did you finish looking at my drawings yet?

Noel: (*Turning away to look at the drawings again*) Read on!

Mark: There were in the same country, shepherds keeping watch over their flock by night. And the angel of the Lord came upon them, and they were sore afraid.

Angel: (*Floating in toward shepherds, upside down*) I'm the one who's going to be sore here.

Mark: What do they mean by "sore afraid"? Noel? Noel? Oh well...And the angel said unto them...

Angel: (*Swinging, speaking a bit frantically*) Fear not; I bring you good tidings of great joy. For unto you is born a Savior, which is Christ the Lord. And this shall be a sign unto you: Ye shall find the babe wrapped in swaddling clothes, lying in a manger.

Noel: (*Without looking up*) Don't sound so frantic, Angel. More joy! Joy!

Angel: I'm try-ing!

    (*Other angels wait on the sidelines with Harold.*)

Mark: Suddenly there was with the angel a multitude of heavenly host . . .

(*Harold is holding them back.*)

Mark: I SAID a multitude of heavenly host.

Noel: Harold! Where are the other angels?

Harold: (*Laughing*) They're waiting in the wings. The wings, get it? Ha! The wings!

Noel: (*At the end of her patience*) Read on!

Mark: And the angels were singing . . .

Angels: Glory to God in the highest and on earth peace, good will toward all.

Noel: Next song! (*To the audience*) Now everyone, I want you all to be the angels. Stand and sing it out with everything you've got. And harmonize this time!

(*Noel leads the singing of "Angels We Have Heard on High," while Gloria plays accompaniment on the piano. Afterward, other angels exit and Mark and Harold sing, "Excelsis deo, deo, daylight come and me wanna go home!"*)

Noel: On with it, already!

Mark: The shepherds said one to another . . .

(*Shepherds aren't in sight. Louder.*)

Mark: The shepherds said one to another . . .

(*Shepherds still aren't around.*)

Mark: (*At the top of his lungs*) Shep-herrrds!

(*Harold pushes shepherds out, each dragging a wooden sheep on wheels or a plush toy sheep.*)

Noel: Where were you guys? You're supposed to be on your way to Bethlehem.

(*Littlest shepherd whispers something in Harold's ear.*)

Noel: Where were they?

Harold: They were on their way to the bathroom-la-hem.

Noel: (*Taking off glasses and rubbing her eyes*) Your line, shepherds. Just do your line.

Shepherds: (*In unison*) Let us now go to Bethlehem and see this wonder which the angels made known unto us.

Mark: And they went with haste . . .

(*Littlest shepherd whispers in Harold's ear.*)

Harold: He wants to know who Haste is.

Mark: (*Continuing*) And found Mary and Joseph and the babe lying in the manger.

Joseph: Mary and Joseph AND the baby all lying in the manger? We won't all fit.

(*Mary and Joseph look at each other, shrug their shoulders and attempt to get into the manger with the doll.*)

Mark: (*Quickly interrupting to save the manger*) I think just the baby is in the manger. (*Resuming narration*) And all of them wondered at those things which were told to them by the shepherds.

Everyone: Wonder, wonder, wonder, wonder.

Mark: But Mary kept all these things and pondered them in her heart.

Mary: Ponder, ponder, ponder.

Mark: And the shepherds returned, praising God.

    (*Shepherds continue to stand there, facing the audience*)

Mark: And the shepherds returned, praising God. (*After no response*) PRAISING GOD!

Noel: Shepherds! Shepherds! (*Top of her lungs*) Shepherrrds!

Harold: (*Pushing the shepherds out, who are dragging their sheep.*) Praise God, praise God, praise God.

    (*Wise ones enter.*)

Mark: Behold, there came wise men from the east saying...

Wise Ones: (*In unison*) Where is he that...

Harold: Hey, two of these wise men are girls!

Wise Girl 1: So what?

Harold: They're not supposed to be girls. They're supposed to be men.

Wise Girl 2: Where are we going to find three wise men in this church?

Harold: (*Pauses and looks around the audience.*) You've got a point there.

Noel: Read on!

Wise Ones: Where is he that is born king of the Jews? For we have seen his star in the east and have come to worship him.

Mark: When Herod the king heard these things, he was troubled. And he sent them to Bethlehem saying...

Herod: Go and search diligently for the child, and when ye have found him, bring me word again that I may come and worship him also.

Harold: Hey! He's trying to trick them!

Noel: Read the script, Mark.

Mark: When they had heard the king they departed, and lo the star went before them 'til it stood over where the young child was.

Noel: OK, next song: "We Three Kings." Ready? Go.

    (*Noel leads the audience in singing "We Three Kings," while Gloria plays accompaniment on the piano. Noel and Harold walk the crowd again, making hand gestures for the crowd to sing louder. When they start into the chorus, Noel stops them and makes them do it again, even louder.*)

Noel: (*Afterward*) You guys sound like a bunch of parents! Oh well. Read on, narrator.

Mark: They saw the young child with Mary, his mother, and fell down and worshiped him.

    (*Wise Ones fall flat on their faces.*)

Mark: And when they had opened their treasures, they presented unto him gifts: gold, and Frankenstein, and myrrh. (*Mark is beaming a mischievous smile.*)

Noel: You can still be replaced, you know.

Mark: Sorry. Just had to see if you were listening. Being warned in a dream that they should not return to Herod, they departed into their own country another way.

(*Wise Ones start to leave the way they came.*)

Mark: Another way!

Wise Ones: (*Embarrassed, they turn and exit another way.*) See ya!

Mark: Sheesh! And they're supposed to be wise.

Noel: Mark!

Mark: Right. Stick to the script. And the Angel appeared to Joseph in a dream saying...

Angel: I don't think this is working!

Noel: That's not in the script!

Angel: Arise and take the child and his mother and flee into Egypt, for Herod will seek the child to destroy him.

Mark: When he arose, he took the child and his mother by night and departed into Egypt.

(*Joseph nudges Mary and whispers in her ear. Both try to pick up the baby to go.*)

Joseph: I want to hold the baby!

Mary: I'm his mother.

Joseph: You always get to hold him. He's mine, too, you know. Noel!

(*Mary and Joseph continue to fight, dropping the doll.*)

Artist: (*Bursting in*) Noel! All the kids who were supposed to help me couldn't wait any longer! Now I'm all alone! I want my drawings!

Shepherds and Angels: (*Running in screaming, everyone saying different things all at once*) Aaah! There's a rat in the costume room! A huge, giant, monstrous, nasty, mean rat! Aaah!

(*Pandemonium breaks loose with everyone tugging on Noel. Mark and Harold begin singing their "Angel Swing" song from page 132. Donkey chases around until its costume comes apart. Someone crashes into the manger. Gloria pounds on the piano to regain attention.*)

Noel: (*Screaming at top of her lungs*) Quiet! Quiet!! QUII-ET!

(*Suddenly the room is silent. Angel, out of her harness, is standing on the front pew, rocking the baby doll in her arms.*)

Angel: Oh, baby Jesus. Shhh. It's OK, it's OK. Don't cry. Shhh. (*She begins to sing quietly.*)

Angel: (*Singing first verse, solo and a cappella*)
Silent night! holy night!
All is calm, all is bright

'Round yon virgin mother and Child,
Holy Infant so tender and mild,
Sleep in heavenly peace,
Sleep in heavenly peace.

(As she sings, Noel's grimace melts. The children are held in awe and slowly sit to hum verse 2 as Angel sings. By verse 3 all join in singing, still a cappella. By verse 4, Noel motions for the audience to join. When song finishes, Angel looks into doll's eyes and strokes his hair.)

Angel: Oh, baby Jesus. Shhh. It's OK. It's OK. Don't cry. They just want to put on a good show. Maybe they don't understand. Maybe they don't understand.

Mark: *(After a long pause, he turns to the audience.)* We're out of time here. Our practice for Christmas is over. Before you go, let's pray: God, you touched the world with the miracle of the Christ child in a stable so long ago. Touch us also in these next hours, that we may know the wonder of your love. Give us a keen sense of focus, that we might not miss the best as we prepare for the rest. Fill us with the joy of the angels, the awe of the shepherds, the desire of the Magi, and a gentle peace that holds our hearts as we hold the Christ child and ponder the meaning of your precious birth. Help us to understand what we're doing all this for anyway. Help us to remember. We pray in Jesus' name. Amen.

Noel: Our recessional song is "Joy to the World," *(mellowed)* and I hope you'll sing it with all the gusto you've got. *(With a false sense of firmness)* And if I catch even one of you not singing, I'm going to have you stay after and sing a solo! Got it? Good!

(Noel leads the audience in singing "Joy to the World." Kids march down the aisle and out the back as they sing the final verse. After all is silent, Mark, Harold, and Noel walk down the aisle arm in arm.)

Mark, Harold, and Noel: *(Singing loudly)* Mark and Harold's angel swing...Lifted Fletcher on her wing...

(Lights fade.)

THE END

DIRECTOR'S NOTES

DIRECTOR'S NOTES

DIRECTOR'S NOTES

DIRECTOR'S NOTES